Outdoors

Worship Feast

25 Experiences of God's Great Earth

Jenny Youngman

Abingdon Press
Nashville

11 12 13 14 15 16 17 18 19 20—10 9 8 7 6 5 4 3 2 1

COVER DESIGN: KEELY MOORE

Index

Contents

Meet the Writers

Jenny Youngman is a singer-songwriter, writer, editor, stay-at-home mom, and pastor's wife. But most of all, she is a worshiper. She is the creator of the WORSHIP FEAST series for youth groups, and she is passionate about creative worship. Jenny leads workshops and worship gatherings for youth retreats and youth worker events. She lives outside of Nashville where she looks for God outdoors, indoors, and everywhere in-between. You can learn more about Jenny and hear her music at *jennyyoungman.com*.

Special thanks to **Gavin Richardson** for his creative worship experiences in Chapter 2. Gavin is a Digital Community Builder for YouthWorker Movement and YouthWorker Circuit. He has ministered with youth for nearly two decades. Gavin often speaks around the country on church communications and community building. He lives in Nashville with his wife Erin, his son Brooks, and two dogs (Coe and Crimson).

Introduction

One of my favorite youth group memories is of the annual summertime worship around a bonfire. We would gather around the fire and give testimonies of how God was working in our lives. We'd talk about sins that we struggled with daily, stuff going on in our families, and dreams for the school year ahead. We would pray and cry together in shared experience. Our youth pastor would talk to us about being "a light" among our friends and making good decisions. Then we would sing the songs "Sanctuary" and "Step by Step" and commit to following Jesus as best we could.

I am almost certain that experience would have been somewhat memorable indoors; but something about the starry sky, the burning flames, the smell of smoke that hung in our clothes for days, the dirt beneath our feet, and the hard benches and tree-stump seats created the lasting memory. It was the getting-out-of-the-ordinary-space kind of setting that helped us participate more fully and expect a God-moment. That's what outdoor worship times do. They help us open our eyes and look for God in the amazing world God created for us to enjoy. Outdoor worship experiences touch all of our senses and provide an awareness of the moment in an unexpected way.

The worship experiences in this book give you some ideas for creating meaningful moments in the lives of your youth. They will teach your youth to look for God everywhere they go and to expect God's presence whether they are on a mountaintop, at an amusement park, or in the middle of a downpour.

The worship experiences are divided into four categories: Water, Wonder, Awareness, and Seasons. Most of the experiences take about thirty minutes, but can be stretched or shortened easily. Each experience includes a Scripture focus, a theme, and a list of items you'll need to stuff in your backpack. The services also suggest songs that relate to the theme of each experience.* It's a good idea to have a guitar (and a guitar player) handy, but you can always sing a cappella.

Additionally, there are some scripted sections to help direct the experiences. The scripted sections are italicized so that you can identify the heart of the teaching. Some people love to have a script; others detest the idea of being told what to say. So know that the italicized segments are intended for you to adapt and use with your own words.

It is my prayer that your group will grow closer and deeper in discipleship as together you look for God in the great outdoors!

—Jenny Youngman

*As always, you should feel free to replace the suggested songs with other appropriate songs that are familiar to your youth.

A *Special Note:* Unless otherwise noted, the Scriptures quoted in this book come from the Common English Bible (CEB). The Common English Bible is a new version that delivers an accurate translation of the ancient texts into English that is clear, familiar, and easy to understand. While this book quotes the Common English Bible and recommends using *THE MESSAGE* in certain situations, any translation of Scripture is suitable for most of these worship experiences.

Chapter 1
Worship With Water

So many great Bible stories center around water:
the crossing of the Red Sea, Noah and the flood,
Jonah washing up onto the shore, Jesus calming the
storm—just to name a few. This chapter of worship
experiences is water-based and is perfect for summer
trips, pool parties, and rainy days.

1 Sunrise on the Beach

"Early in the morning, Jesus stood on the shore, but the disciples didn't realize it was Jesus" (John 21:4).

Scripture: John 21:1-14

Theme: Seeing Jesus

Supplies: Pack a cooler with some breakfast food (such as ready-to-bake biscuits, breakfast meats, bagels and cream cheese, fruit, yogurt, and cereal with milk); picnic blankets or camping chairs; drinks (such as juice, milk, and coffee); plates, cups, and napkins. A guitar (and someone to play it) is recommended. If possible, take plates and pitchers so youth can serve one another.

Overview: What better way to experience the story of Jesus making breakfast for the disciples following his resurrection then to reenact the Scripture passage and join Jesus for breakfast on the beach. Ask your group to meet just before dawn at the beach or a riverbank or lakeshore. Lead a time of worship and then eat breakfast together right there on the shore. If possible, gather around a fire. If not, cook on a grill or provide breakfast foods that don't need to be cooked.

Opening Words: Say something like, *"Soon after Jesus had shown himself to his disciples, Simon Peter, Thomas, and several other disciples went out to fish; it's what they knew how to do. To say the least, the events of the previous days had been a roller coaster. Jesus, their Lord, teacher, and friend had been betrayed and crucified. And just when they believed he was dead, that all hope was lost, Jesus rose from the dead and appeared to them. Experiencing exhilaration so soon after* despair surely was emotionally exhausting. So these young men felt the need to get back to something familiar—fishing.

"Early in the morning, after a frustrating night during which they caught nothing, the disciples noticed a man on the shore whom they did not recognize. He told them to cast their nets on the other side of the boat. When they followed these simple instructions, the disciples caught more fish than they could handle. They soon realized that the man on the shore was Jesus. Peter was so excited that he jumped out of the boat into the water and swam to shore.

"When the rest of the disciples brought the boat to shore, Jesus greeted them with breakfast—bread and fish that he had cooked on a fire. This morning we're going to imagine that this shore is the beach where Jesus ate with his friends. In fact, we're going to consider ourselves as those friends and eat with Jesus right here. As we sit on the shore, watching and listening to the water and feeling the breeze on our faces (and possibly smelling smoke from the fire), let's turn our eyes to see Jesus among us this morning."

Sing Praise: Sing these songs that emphasize spending time with Jesus or the glory of God's creation (see note on page 6):

✳ "For the Glory of It All" (David Crowder)
✳ "Open the Eyes of My Heart"
 (Paul Baloche)
✳ "From the Rising of the Sun"
 (anonymous)

Scripture Reading: Ask for some volunteers to read aloud **John 21:1-14.**

Activity: Looking for Jesus

Say something like: "*The disciples didn't know the man on the shore was Jesus until they lifted the net from the right side of the boat and found it overflowing with fish. At that point they knew it was their Lord; they had eyes to see. Their despair and exhaustion from the events of the previous days, their uncertainty about what would happen next, and their frustration after a night of failed fishing* had the disciples looking down. They didn't have eyes to look up and see what else God might do. We get like that sometimes, too. We become lost in our frustrations and miss seeing Jesus right in front of us. For the next few minutes I want you to take a prayer walk along the shore and pray for eyes to see how Jesus is with you, around you, and at work in your life. Look along the water's edge and collect items that might remind you to keep your eyes open to see Jesus. Once you have gathered a few items, find a place to sit and pray, continue walking along the beach, or find a quiet spot to stand and gaze at the water. Then imagine Peter jumping out of the boat and swimming to Jesus.*"

Before sending the youth out on their walks, say a prayer such as the following: "*Lord, we want eyes to see you. We know you are all around us—behind, before, beside, within. Open our eyes and help us to see you always. Amen.*"

While the youth take their prayer walks, prepare your breakfast table or picnic. If possible, light a fire. As best you can, create a sense of hospitality. If possible, set out plates of food and pitchers of drinks so the youth can serve one another. Make the space inviting and comfortable with picnic blankets or camping chairs.

After about ten minutes, call the youth back from their walks and invite them to breakfast. As everyone gets their food and finds a seat, begin a conversation about the items they brought back as reminders of Jesus' presence. Ask for volunteers to tell about their items. Remind youth that Jesus and the disciples shared breakfast on the beach at sunrise, just as you all are gathered now. Talk about what it would be like if Jesus were sitting there with you eating, talking, and laughing together.

Then say something like: *"The events surrounding Jesus' trial, death, and resurrection were traumatic, surprising, and exciting. Jesus' disciples had no idea what else might happen or what their future held. But they knew that their friend—their Lord— died and then came back to life. And there he was on the shore at sunrise hosting a meal for them. Jesus was present with his disciples when they needed him most, and he is present with us today. We simply need to pay attention to the ways we can see Christ among us."*

Closing: After everyone has finished eating, gather in a circle. Sing together again "Open the Eyes of My Heart" (or another song from earlier). Then, invite volunteers to pray around the circle.

2 At a Well

"Everyone who drinks this water will be thirsty again, but whoever drinks from the water that I will give will never be thirsty again. The water that I give will become in those who drink it a spring of water that bubbles up into eternal life" (John 4:13-14).

Scripture: John 4:1-15

Theme: Life-giving Water

Supplies: Collect some inexpensive, Nalgene-style water bottles, one for each student; pack a bag with colored permanent markers, glitter glue, and paint pens; and bring a few gallons of water, enough for youth to fill their bottles during the service.

Overview: The story of the Samaritan woman at the well paints a beautiful picture of Jesus' compassion and grace. If possible, gather your youth around a well and invite them into the story of a woman who finds identity, belonging, and new life as she talks to Jesus (someone her culture said she shouldn't have been talking to), and then runs to her village to spread the good news.

Opening Words: Say something like, *"Most of the time, when we want a drink of water, we go to the cabinet, get out a cup or glass, and turn on the faucet or push the button on the fridge. We don't have to work very hard to quench our physical thirst. But during Jesus' time (and in lots of places around the world today), you had to hike to the village well, fill water buckets or jars, and then carry them back to your house. Our Bible story takes place at a well like this one.*

"Jesus had been traveling from Judea to Galilee. He had been walking from town to town, so you can imagine his need to stop and rest a while and get a drink of water. Since he couldn't simply stop at a nearby water fountain, he found the next best thing—Jacob's well. As Jesus sat by the well resting, a woman came to draw water. This trip to the well would change her life forever."

Sing Praise: (see note on page 6)

✳ "Jesus Messiah" (Chris Tomlin)
✳ "Come and Listen" (David Crowder)

Scripture Reading: Ask for some volunteers to read aloud John 4:1-15.

Activity: Living Water

Say something like: *"This Samaritan woman experiences a life-changing moment because of her trip to Jacob's well. She had been looking in all the wrong places to find the love for which her soul longed. At the well Jesus offered her an everlasting love that would fill up her soul and make her whole. Though Jesus named the sin in her life, the woman ended up bringing her entire village to meet Jesus: the one who knew everything she did, loved her anyway, and met her deepest longings. Think about the ways that Jesus gives you the longings of your heart: belonging, forgiveness, abundant life. Think about the things or places or people that you turn to when you feel alone or in need. Imagine Jesus offering you the kind of water that would give you life—real, bubbling, meaningful life. Have you taken Jesus up on that offer? Have you taken a drink of his life-giving water?"*

Invite the group to decorate and write **John 4:14** on their bottles: "Whoever drinks from the water that I will give will never be thirsty again." Encourage youth to be creative and express their personality as they decorate their water bottles.

Now ask youth to fill their bottles using the water you brought with you. After everyone has filled his or her bottle, explain that you will read aloud the Scripture again. Invite the youth, as you read, to take a long drink from their bottles and meditate on the soul-quenching water that Jesus offered the Samaritan woman and also offers us today. Read the Scripture three times, pausing briefly between each reading.

Closing: Gather in a circle around the well and pray together, asking God to quench your thirst with Jesus' life-giving water. Invite your youth to accept Jesus' offer to never be thirsty again.

3 At a Swimming Pool

"Wash me completely clean of my guilt; purify me from my sin!" (Psalm 51:2).

Scripture: Psalm 51:1-15

Theme: Forgiveness of Sins

Supplies: None needed

Overview: Psalm 51 is the prayer that David prayed after his affair with Bathsheba. You can hear the depth of his grief and his longing to be made clean. In his prayer David admits his wrongdoing, seeks forgiveness, demonstrates true repentance, and begs for a clean slate. We can all relate to guilt, shame, and the longing for a do-over. Invite your youth to be washed by the water and made clean by the Spirit—literally. Gather around a swimming pool to read the psalm, then jump in together and wash your sins away. (Lead this worship time near the shallow end so that nonswimmers can stand up and walk from side to side.)

Opening Words: Say something like, *"As we spend the day at the pool, let's take a moment to talk about water. Water is life-giving, cleansing, and refreshing. Water is cool relief from a hot summer day. Today we're going to read a psalm that David wrote after he had committed adultery and plotted murder. He was laden with guilt and devastated with remorse. His psalm is a prayer to be washed clean and purified from his wrongdoings. This swimming pool will symbolize and mark for us a prayer journey of forgiveness from sin."*

Sing Praise: (see note on page 6)

☀ "Grace Like Rain" (Todd Agnew)
☀ "Amazing Grace" (John Newton)

Scripture Reading: Read aloud, or ask for volunteers to read aloud, **Psalm 51:1-15.**

Now say something like: *"David made some major mistakes. Out of arrogance and pride he rationalized committing both adultery and murder. This guy was chosen by God to be the king, and he still fell short of who God had called him to be. He was overcome with and submitted to temptation; then he went to extreme lengths to cover up his sin. That's how it can be with temptation and sin. Take lying, for example. You lie once and then you have to lie again to cover up the original lie. Pretty soon you have constructed a story that is actually just a string of lies—and sometimes you can't even remember how it all began.*

"Maybe you've been where David was emotionally. Hopefully none of you have committed adultery or murder (and if you have, we should talk!); but each of us struggles with his or her burden of sin and temptation. Maybe it's anger, or greed, or doing anything to be popular—no matter the cost. Maybe it's drinking or pushing sexual boundaries too far or deceiving your parents to get your way or the things you want. Maybe it's apathy or laziness. Whatever your struggle, I want you to imagine David's heart as he wrote today's psalm. He had hit rock bottom. All he could do was surrender to God's mercy and pray for a do-over."

Activity: Wash Clean in the Water

Say something like: *"Take a minute to think about your most difficult struggles and temptations. What brings you to God in search of forgiveness? As you think about your personal struggles, listen again to David's psalm. (Read* **Psalm 51:1-15** *aloud again.) Now look at this big pool of water. Imagine that where we are standing now represents a place of guilt and that the space on the other side of the water represents freedom from that guilt and a new beginning. One at a time, as we swim or walk across to the other side of the water, we will be "washed clean" of our guilt and come out in a place of joy and freedom. Before you jump in, let's all say together verse 2: "Wash me completely clean of my guilt; purify me from my sin!"*

Ask the youth to line up along the water's edge. When students reach the other side, they should get out and wait for the rest of the group to cross over, with you as the last one. Lead a closing prayer on the "side of joy and freedom."

Closing: When you reach the other side of the pool, ask the youth to join hands in a circle. Lead a popcorn prayer and invite youth to lift up their thoughts as they feel led to do so. Close your worship experience by reading aloud **Psalm 51:8–10.**

4 In a Spring Rain

"Let them shout, and shout, and shout!
   Oh, oh, let them sing!" (Psalm 65:13,
THE MESSAGE).

Scripture: Psalm 65:2-13

Theme: Praise God in Creation

Supplies: Ahead of time ask youth to bring umbrellas, rain coats, rain boots, and a change of clothes for when they go back inside. Also print the psalm on sheets of paper or note cards and laminate or place them inside plastic bags so that each student has a copy of the psalm.

Overview: Psalm 65 is a declaration that calls all of nature to praise God. A rainy day is the perfect time for youth to celebrate the God of creation. *THE MESSAGE* uses fun language to remind us that God calls the earth to dance with praise. The rains come to fill the rivers and cause nature to break out in beautiful colors. Stand with your group in the middle of the rain and join with all of nature to praise God's faithfulness and beauty.

Opening Words: Say something like, *"Today we're going to join with all of nature in shouting out praises to God. We're going to feel the rain on our heads and imagine that beautiful spring growth is sprouting up in our lives. And we'll focus on God's perfect timing and God's faithfulness during each season.*

"Think about the fact that the spring rains know exactly when to water the earth in preparation for May flowers. Think about the perfect way that the moon dances around the earth and the earth around the sun. Think about the buds that push through the ground and reach upward to their Maker as if to praise."

Sing Praise: (see note on page 6)

* ✳ "Lifesong" (Casting Crowns)
* ✳ "All Creatures of Our God and King" (David Crowder)

Activity: Just Praising in the Rain

Turn to **Psalm 65:2-13**, preferably in THE MESSAGE. Gather youth in a circle and allow each person to read aloud a verse at a time. Then read the psalm again, one verse at a time, but this time ask the youth to shout as loud as they can (while still being audible).

Now ask the youth to close their eyes and stand in silence as the rain falls on and around them. Invite them to reflect on these questions one at a time:

1. How does your life praise your Maker?
2. What season of life are you in right now? (*a season of change, a season of growth, a season of complacency, a season of discernment, and so forth*)
3. How could you join in the dance of creation, declaring worship and praise to the God who created it all?

Lead the youth to read aloud the psalm once more. Encourage them to see themselves as part of the beauty that God created and to worship the God who formed them so perfectly.

Closing: Say a prayer of praise and then invite the youth to celebrate God's beautiful creation by running around in the rain, splashing in puddles, and feeling the rain on their faces.

5 In a River

"I'm baptizing you here in the river, turning your old life in for a kingdom life. His baptism—a holy baptism by the Holy Spirit—will change you from the inside out" (Mark 1:8, THE MESSAGE).

Scripture: Mark 1:4-8

Theme: Remember Your Baptism

Supplies: None needed

Overview: If you have a nearby river or stream, gather at its banks with your youth. Ask them to put their feet in the water and to imagine what it might have been like when John the Baptist called people into the river to repent and be baptized. You may have several youth who were baptized as infants, some who were baptized as children, and still others who have not yet been baptized. While this will not be a baptism ritual, you can offer an opportunity to remember for those who have been baptized and an opportunity to dream for those who have not yet been baptized but may be thinking about taking that step.

Opening Words: Say something like, *"When John the Baptist came out of the wilderness and invited people into the waters, he got everyone's attention. Some probably stopped and stared. Others probably ran into the waters begging for a second chance at life. Still others probably scoffed and were annoyed at John's arrogance—what gave him the right to go around baptizing anyone? As we stand here at this river (or stream), let's imagine that we are with the crowd gathered there with John the Baptist. These are people who believed that God would send the Messiah very soon; but they were not sure who* he would be or what he would look like. And they were not certain that this strange looking guy from the desert was truly worthy of the call to announce the Messiah's coming. Still, we learn from the Scripture that he called people to repent of their sins and turn toward God and that many believed him, flocked to him, and were baptized by him.

"Some of you were baptized as babies, others as children, and some of you may not have been baptized yet. Today, for those of you who have been baptized, take time to remember that ritual, feel the waters, and reaffirm your commitment to Christ. For those of you who haven't been baptized yet, we'll dream together about when you might be ready to take that step."

Sing Praise: (see note on page 6)

✸ "Dance in the River" (Chris Tomlin)
✸ "Create in Me a Clean Heart" (Keith Green)

Scripture Reading: Read aloud **Mark 1:4-8**, preferably from *THE MESSAGE*.

Activity: Changed From the Inside Out

Ask youth to stand near a shallow part at the bank of the river or stream. When everyone's gathered close, ask them to take off their socks and shoes.

Say something like: *"Imagine that you're going about your business when some guy walks right out of the woods and hollers at you to repent and be baptized. He tells you that someone is coming who will change you from the inside out. He says that your whole life is about to change—everything you know now will be different when you meet the One who is coming soon.*

"You are excited, intrigued, wary, suspicious, open, closed-off, hopeful . . . you want what he says to be true. You want to be changed. You want forgiveness and a new chance at life. You want to live for something important. You want to be part of a bigger story. You want this Holy Spirit he talks about to make you new and give you purpose.

"I'm going to read again from Mark, Chapter 1. As I read, I want you to put your feet into the water. As you feel the water on your skin, imagine that you are among the crowds entering the water in response to John the Baptist's calls. Pray a silent prayer of confession and repentance, seeking forgiveness for any sin in your life. (Read aloud the Scripture.)

"Now take a few more steps into the water. I'll read the Bible passage again, and this time I want you to pray silently that you would be changed from the inside out. If you were baptized as a baby or a child, I want you to remember the covenant your parents made with God on your behalf. Remember the promises of God. Remember that God has claimed you as God's own beloved child. If you haven't been baptized yet, I want you to pray about what is holding you back. Pray for trust and faith in God's goodness and faithfulness. (Read the Scripture again.)

"Take a few more steps into the water. This time I want you to reach down and pick up a small stone or rock that you can take away from this experience. This stone will be a symbol of the river's water that we stand in today. It will remind you that God has made you new and changed you from the inside out. Listen as I read the Scripture passage one last time. (Read the Scripture a final time.)

"Now, let's have some fun in this water that represents our new life in Christ." (As you say these words, splash some water towards the group. Hopefully this will invite a splashfest.)

Closing: After a few minutes of splashing around, call the youth away from the water and gather in a circle. Ask for some volunteers to tell what it means to them to be claimed by God. Ask those who can remember to tell about their baptism experience. Join hands and lead a prayer of thanksgiving for the gift of baptism into the kingdom of God. Thank God for the gift of new life and pray that your group may be filled with the Holy Spirit and lead others to Jesus as John the Baptist did.

6 Lakeside

"Jesus said to Simon, 'Don't be afraid. From now on, you will be fishing for people.' As soon as they brought the boats to shore, they left everything and followed Jesus" (Luke 5:10b-11).

Scripture: Luke 5:1-11

Theme: Following Jesus

Supplies: Provide a mini notebook, pen or pencil, and a Bible or printout of **Luke 5:1-11** for each person. Also cut a supply of four-inch squares of cheesecloth, enough for at least one or two per person. (You can usually find cheesecloth in the baking aisle). You'll also need thinline permanent markers, a large fishing net with two or three buckets, and a small bell.

Overview: Jesus asked his disciples to leave everything they knew at the edge of the lake and go with him to begin his ministry. They didn't have time to think about all they were leaving behind. They didn't have time to think about whether or not this was a good decision. They heard Jesus' call, trusted him, and dropped their nets to follow him. Invite your youth on this journey with Jesus by meeting at a nearby lake. Help them to think about what it means to join the ranks of the disciples, leaving their old lives behind and following Jesus.

Youth will make a journal entry in their mini notebooks, reflecting on what in their lives they need to leave behind in order to truly follow Jesus. They'll take a prayer walk during which they will decide what they must leave behind to make a commitment or recommit themselves to choosing a life with Jesus.

Opening Words: Say something like, *"Here we are, like Jesus and his disciples in today's Scripture, standing next to a lake. Imagine having been fishing on a boat and then nearing shore to find Jesus preaching to the crowds. The disciples hadn't had much luck catching fish that time out. Before they knew it, Jesus was in their boat telling them to push out a bit— and they felt compelled to do what he said. They also sensed that something bigger than anything they'd ever experienced was about to happen.*

"Jesus called his disciples to leave their nets and become fishers of men and women—to catch people with God's love. And that's what he calls us to do today. When we follow Jesus, we leave behind our personal desires and aspirations and choose his path for our lives. Today we're going to think about what we're leaving behind when Jesus calls us to follow him. And we're going to dream about what a life with Jesus looks like."

Sing Praise: (see note on page 6)

✳ "You Are Worthy of My Praise" (Jeremy Camp)

Scripture Reading: Read aloud **Luke 5:1-11**.

Activity: Follow Me

Hand out mini notebooks, pens, and Bibles or print outs of **Luke 5:1-11**. Instruct youth to spread out (obviously, they should remain in your sight). When they are situated, youth should write or draw any thoughts they have about what it means to follow Jesus and what they must leave behind to do so. Encourage them to choose the creative expression that feels best for them—journaling, writing songs or poetry, drawing pictures, illustrating ideas, and so

on. Ask them to read the Scripture passage a few times, then reflect on what Jesus might be asking them through the story: *What if you were present on the shore that day? What if Jesus called you to leave your "nets" and follow him? How can you follow Jesus at school, at home, and in all aspects of your life?*

While the youth are working, set up a prayer station near the water. Lay out the fishing net and anchor it with the buckets. Lay around the squares of cheesecloth and markers, making sure they won't blow away.

After about ten minutes, ring a bell and reassemble the youth. Ask for volunteers to tell about what they wrote or drew. Remind the youth that Jesus told those first disciples to leave their nets—the nets represented their careers, their livelihoods, and everything they knew—to follow him.

When the conversation slows, explain that you have set up a prayer station and youth should go and write on a square of cheesecloth the thing in their lives that would represent their "nets." After a minute or two, ask them to drop the squares in a bucket and then pray a silent prayer committing or recommitting to follow Jesus.

When everyone is finished, read aloud the Scripture passage a final time. Say something like: *"We leave this lake to follow Jesus. We leave behind what we knew before—those things that hindered us following Jesus—and choose the road that Jesus leads us down. We give ourselves to share in Jesus' ministry in the world."* Also pray for strength and courage to follow Jesus on days when the road isn't easy.

Closing: Sing together the oldie but goodie, "I Have Decided to Follow Jesus."

🔯 Bonus: In Sight of a Waterfall

"But let justice roll down like waters,
and righteousness like an ever-flowing stream" (Amos 5:24).

Scripture: Amos 5:23-25

Theme: Justice

Supplies: Purchase small (or large if you have the money) canvases (at a craft store) that are already stretched around a wood frame (so you won't need tables or easels), along with a variety of oil paints, pastels, and brushes. Also collect pieces of cardboard to use as palettes. Bring large trash bags for cleanup and small bags for dirty paint brushes. Also have available a few different Bible versions.

Overview: The prophet Amos's words in 5:23-25 have been used in many famous speeches. The word picture of justice rolling through our world eliminating all of the oppression and washing away the scars of poverty helps us understand that God is serious about justice. As you view a waterfall with your group, help them dream about a future of justice for all God's people. Help them dream about how God might have work for them to do for the cause of justice.

The youth will paint pictures of a waterfall near where you meet. The artwork will be a form of prayer as they create with their hands and dream with their hearts about the work God has for them to do to bring justice and righteousness into the world like a waterfall.

Opening Words: Say something like, *"Waterfalls demonstrate the power and force of moving water. The rivers flow and rush and cascade down the sides of cliffs as they burst forward. The beauty of falls like this one show us how magnificently creative our God is. Falls like this also help us imagine what the prophet Amos might have meant when he said, 'Let justice roll on like a river.' Today we're going to dream about how God might use us to work for justice in the world with a force like this waterfall as it pushes the water further ahead."*

Sing Praise: (see note on page 6)

✳ "Justice Will Roll Down" (Sandra McCracken)

Scripture Reading: Read aloud, or ask volunteers to read **Amos 5:23-25** from a few different translations.

Activity: Working for Justice

Say something like: *"These words from Amos weren't meant just for his original audience. His words are for us today, and they tell us something about the heart of God. God hates oppression and poverty and injustice. In fact, our Scripture passage tells us that God doesn't even want our worship unless we are committed to the work of God's justice in the world. A well-known pastor and justice advocate writes about a seminary project in which a friend literally cut out every Bible verse that mentioned justice and oppression. When the group finished cutting out all of the related verses, the Bible was in shreds. There was little left to read. His story demonstrates that God tells us what God cares about on every page of God's Word: feeding the hungry, freeing the oppressed, caring for the least of these among us.*

"Amos paints a picture of justice sweeping across the earth, wiping out all forms of injustice and oppression. This waterfall helps us visualize that action. The force of this water keeps the river moving—over the cliff and down the river bank. The water never stops moving. It is always rushing forward with its current. God calls us to be a current of justice in today's society. In a world where children are sold into slavery, where women are kidnapped and sold to brothels, where kids look for food in city dumps, where young people don't have time or money to attend school because they must walk for miles to draw the daily buckets of water or beg for coins in the city, and where homeless people are forced out of the city or hidden away—God calls us to bring God's justice and hope.

"Just as this waterfall is a thing of beauty that protests the dark and ugly places in the world, we're going to create artwork as an act of prayer and a protest to injustice. Using a blank canvas, paint a picture of this waterfall. As you paint, be in prayer about how God might lead you into the current of justice and use you to respond to poverty and oppression. Pray for the imprisoned and impoverished persons around the world. Meditate on God's justice flowing through the world like the water that you are painting. Also include the words of **Amos 5:24** on your canvas."

Hand out the canvas boards and help everyone set up with their brushes and paints. If possible, play some instrumental music or favorite songs that speak to God's justice and Christian compassion. Begin the painting time with a prayer something like this: "God, you create beautiful things to remind us that you are all about beauty. There is no room in your world for ugliness, destruction, despair, violence, or oppression. You call us to move like a mighty stream—

*overcoming the ugly with your beauty. Give us eyes
to see injustice and the courage to make a difference.
Come be with us as we use our hands to create a
thing of beauty."*

As the youth finish their paintings, clean the
palettes and brushes. Set all the paintings in a
row so that everyone can see one another's
work. Invite volunteers to tell about what they
painted and their experience in prayer.
Encourage the youth to continue thinking about how to
bring beauty to ugly situations. Inspire them to seek out
acts of justice and compassion. As a group, commit to
focus on seeking justice.

Closing: Say a prayer of thanksgiving for all that God has
done and will do to eliminate oppression and injustice in
the world. Pray again for courage to do the hard work of
seeking justice and being the generation that will usher
in the justice and righteousness about which Amos spoke
in today's Scripture passage.

❈ Bonus: On a Boat

"Then Peter got out of the boat and was walking on the water toward Jesus. But when Peter saw the strong wind, he became frightened. As he began to sink, he shouted, 'Lord, rescue me!'" (Matthew 14:29b-30).

Scripture: Matthew 14:22-30

Theme: Trust

Supplies: You will need a boat, life jackets for everyone, tubes, skis, wakeboards, coolers with snacks, drinks, and lunch. Be sure a certified lifeguard is present.

Overview: Peter takes us on a roller coaster of emotion in Matthew 14:22-30—his excitement at seeing Jesus walk on the water, his disbelief that it could truly be Jesus, his test to prove that it *was* Jesus, his faith, his doubt, and ultimately his belief. Peter's journey to belief represents the road we all take. Begin your time on the boat with a worship experience to help youth trust Jesus to (metaphorically) walk on water in their lives.

Perhaps you'll be tubing, skiing, or wakeboarding during the day. Water sports can help the youth feel like they are literally walking on water—wind in their hair, water splashing on their faces, soaring on top of the water—all feelings that are experienced in a life of trusting Jesus.

Opening Words: Say something like, *"Doesn't it feel great out here on the water? The wind is so fresh and the water is so peaceful. Can you imagine being out here on*

the boat and then seeing someone walk toward us? What would you think if you saw a man approaching our boat—walking on top of the water? We would probably all be a little freaked out, right?

"Today we're going to hear the Bible story and reflect on what a life of trusting Jesus feels like. We're also going to take a lap on skis or on the tube and trust the rope to keep us up."

Tell the Story (from Peter's perspective): "We had been with Jesus all day. He had said the most amazing things to the crowds. Everyone wanted to be close to him and listen to his teachings. What an honor to be among his disciples. He sent us out on a boat while he finished up with the crowds. I wasn't sure when we would see him again, but it was nice to take a break from the chaos and be out on the water relaxing with my friends and brothers. The waves were strong, but they were almost therapeutic, rocking us to sleep.

"Suddenly it was almost dawn. As we stretched and yawned and wiped our eyes, we noticed something strange in the distance. It looked like someone was walking toward us, which wouldn't have been unusual—except for the fact that we were way out on the water. Who has the power to walk on the water? My friends were sure that we were seeing ghosts, and we were even a little afraid.

"Turns out, it was Jesus, though we didn't notice right away. We barely believed it even when he identified himself! I needed some proof: 'Jesus,' I said, 'if it's you, tell me to get out of this boat and walk to you.' Surely no ghost would have called out to me or helped me walk on water. Then Jesus called, 'Come on out'—and the most amazing thing happened. You will not believe this, but I was actually walking on top of the water. With my eyes on Jesus, I literally walked toward him as if the water were a firm road! I was so excited! But then the waves swelled up around me and I became afraid. The minute I took my eyes off of Jesus, I felt fear and I dropped into the water. 'Save me, Jesus!' I cried out.

"True to form, Jesus reached out his hand and pulled me right out of the water. Once we were inside the boat, the wind and the waves died down. 'Why didn't you have faith in me, Peter? You know you can trust me to care for you,' Jesus said. 'You know that when you believe you can do amazing things. You have to believe.'

"Everyone else on the boat was amazed at Jesus' power. We all agreed that he is the Son of God and that we should put all of our trust in him. When he looked out at the water, we smiled at one another, amazed that we are a part of his great work.

"That's how it is for you, too. If you call yourself a Jesus-follower, you get to be part of this amazing, walking-on-water-kind-of-stuff. But you've got to trust him. Jesus has great things for you to do. Believe him. Trust him. Go to him."

Activity: Walking on Water

Now spend some time playing on the water using the skis or the tubes. Before the youth jump in, share this blessing over them: *"Go and walk on the water. Feel the wind in your hair and the water splashing on your face. This is what it can feel like when you trust Jesus."*

After everyone has had an opportunity to experience the rush of the breeze and the water, gather the youth back in the boat and talk about how easy or hard it is to trust Jesus in our daily lives. Remind youth of the great things that Jesus has planned for them to do in the days ahead and invite them to trust that Jesus will give them all the strength and courage they need.

Closing: Lead in a prayer for your group that Jesus would call them all to "walk on water" and to do amazing works in the community and in the world. Then, get those kids back out on the water and enjoy God's good world!

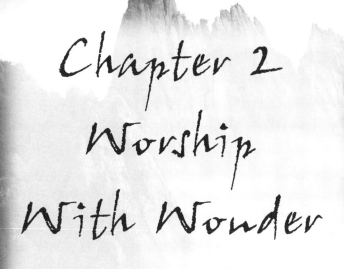

Chapter 2
Worship
With Wonder

God created some amazing wonders in this world—
the stars, the mountains, rainbows—
God's beauty is everywhere. Help your youth
experience God outside in the beauty of creation as
they worship the God of amazing wonders.

7 On a Mountaintop

"He went up onto a mountain by himself to pray" (Matthew 14:23).

Scripture: Matthew 14:23

Theme: Retreat to Pray

Supplies: You will need fabric squares in a variety of colors and types. Also have available string or rope, along with safety pins and permanent markers. Youth should bring backpacks with water, Bible, snacks, and lunch.

Overview: Perhaps no other place is more suited for a prayerful retreat than the mountains. Jesus often retreated to pray. After feeding the five thousand, Jesus went up into the mountains without his disciples or anyone else for a time of prayer. Give your youth the gift of prayer time on the mountain—away from cell phones, social media, homework, and stress. You'll create prayer flags that mark a moment of worship and prayer for the youth.

Opening Words: Say something like, *"After one of the largest and most significant miracles in Jesus' ministry, feeding more than five thousand people, he sent everyone away—even his closest friends—so that he could spend time resting and praying. Imagine being the center of attention for so many people—people who are climbing all over one another to hear what you have to say, to receive blessings, to be healed, to draw closer to God. Christ was many things to many people; but at the end of the day, Christ was fully human and with that, humanly tired. So he climbed a mountain to rest and pray.*

"Here on our mountain today, we have moved away from our daily, busy world. The hundreds of people on our cell phones,

the thousands of people on Facebook, or even the dozen or so of our closest friends can't reach us here. We too are going to follow Christ's example to retreat and spend time in prayer with God."

Sing Praise: (see note on page 6)

✳ "Mighty to Save" (Ben Fielding, Reuben Morgan)
✳ "Sanctuary" (Jaci Valasquez)

Scripture Reading: Read aloud **Matthew 14:23**.

Activity: Prayer Flags

Say something like: "*In mountaineering it is customary to carry along a flag or two. These flags have many purposes and meanings. Some flags are country flags, used to 'lay claim' to a mountain for the climber's country. Some are left as messages to whomever comes next to that location. Some are documentation of who's been there and why. Some are even prayer flags. The practice of prayer flags is prominent today in the Himalayan Buddhist tradition: The idea is that a flag blown by the wind would carry prayers across the land. Using flags for communication and identification is nothing new. Ships use flags to declare their identity, and the church has its own Christian flag.*

"*Today we'll take time to pray and create prayer flags that mark the place of our time with God and then share with others about our time of resting with God on the mountain.*"

Instruct the youth to take a piece of cloth and a marker or two. Invite them to move to a quiet spot on the mountain (but not so far that you can't walk around and see them). They should also take their backpacks and

individual supplies. Explain that they will spend time alone and in prayer with God. Then as they feel led, they should write or draw on the fabric pieces some of the words and images that reflect their time on the mountain. *Hint:* Suggest they begin by first drawing a simple image on the fabric, perhaps a cross in the center.

If necessary, use the following leading questions to help youth focus:

* What are your struggles?
* What are your joys?
* What things are important to you?
* What causes you pain?
* What are the things you've left behind?
* What awaits you at home?
* Where is God in your chaos?

Set a time and place for youth to meet back. When the youth have gathered together again, pull out the rope you brought and attach their flags to the rope using the safety pins. String the rope between one or two trees, or maybe three, depending on your surroundings. As youth stand near the flags, ask a few of them to point out their flags and talk about their experience of resting and praying.

Closing: Ask if someone would like to read aloud a prayer from his or her flag. If not, ask everyone to share one meaningful word from his or her personal prayer time. Then lead in a group prayer that your youth would continue to retreat and pray in the days ahead.

Note: Check with the park ranger before leaving the flags. If the flags are made of lightweight paper, then they may litter the mountainside after a few days or a week. You may need to take them down or return and retrieve them after a few days.

8 In a Cave

"[Elijah] got up, ate and drank his fill, and set out. Nourished by that meal, he walked forty days and nights, all the way to the mountain of God, to Horeb. When he got there, he crawled into a cave and went to sleep" (1 Kings 19:8-9, THE MESSAGE).

Scripture: Matthew 6:5-8

Theme: Self-revealed

Supplies: You will need a candle, a lighter, and flashlights.

Overview: It's scary, and often difficult, to acknowledge the darkest parts of our soul and being. Sometimes we hide from those places, covering them with business, gadgets, television, sports, or a host of other distractions. Being alone with God is truly tough and can be unsettling. So, many times we do what we can to avoid being there. For this experience, take your youth into a cave—one that has a room or space where all participants can sit comfortably.

Opening Words: Say something like, *"It is said that the scariest place to be is alone with God, because it is when we are alone with God that God reveals to us our true selves, including those dark and scary places in our lives that we'd rather ignore. But it is also in moments of solitude with God that God reveals to us the wonderful plan for our lives.*

"During the early years of the church, a group of men and women escaped into the desert to flee the distractions of 'normal life' and to be more fully present with God. These folks are historically referred to as the Desert Fathers and Mothers.

They often lived in caves, much like this one, and had very eccentric lives compared to others of their time. Their stories and sayings are a unique part of our church history. A story about one of the Desert Fathers, Abba Marcarius, goes like this:

Abba Marcarius said to his brothers, "When mass has ended in the church, flee, my brothers." And when one of the brothers said to him, "Father, in this solitude where can we further flee?" And he put his finger up to his mouth saying, "This is what I would have you flee." And so he would go into his cell and shut the door and sit there alone.

"It was not enough for Abba Marcarius to retreat to the desert away from the busyness of the culture. He sat alone in his personal 'cell' (what monks often called their cave dwellings) in silence. He wanted to eliminate anything that would distract him from time alone with God."

Sing Praise: (see note on page 6)

☀ "Peace Be Still" (Stephen Iverson)
☀ "It Is Well With My Soul" (Horatio Spafford)

Scripture Reading: Read aloud **Matthew 6:5-8**. Or, read instead **John 15:4**.

Activity: Be Still and Know

Say something like: *"We are going to open up ourselves to God without speaking or looking around. Find a spot where you have the space to sit or stretch out comfortably. Once everyone is settled, we will turn off our flashlights, and I will light a candle. Then I will read a prayer that describes a posture for you to take with your hands. After the prayer, take a moment to soak up the solitude and allow God to fill you."*

Adapted From the Prayer of St. Patrick

Christ with me (*hands on side*)
Christ before me (*hands forward*)
Christ behind me (*hands backward*)
Christ within me (*hands on heart*)
Christ beneath me (*hands lower than legs or feet*)
Christ above me (*hands stretched above head or on head*)
Christ at my right (*hands on right side*)
Christ at my left (*hands on left side*)
Christ in the heart of everyone who thinks of me (*hands on side of head*)
Christ in the mouth of everyone who speaks of me (*hands on lips*)
Christ in every eye that sees me (*hands on eyes*)
Christ in every ear that hears me (*hands on ears*)
Christ with me.

Allow the group to sit in silence for as long as you feel comfortable. If you have an MP3 player, you might play some prayerful music while youth sit quietly in reflection. Depending on your group and the cave, you may have to remind them not to move around in the darkness. When you turn on the flashlights again, ask youth to point their flashlights downward to allow time for everyone's eyes to adjust.

Note: Some caves have fragile ecosystems and may have rules against fires or smoke, eliminating the use of a candle. You can always use a battery-operated candle—and you won't have to worry about hot wax.

Debrief this prayer experience by discussing the questions on the following page.

✴ Was it difficult to be completely quiet and to clear your mind?

✴ Were you scared of the darkness, of feeling alone?

✴ Did you feel closer to God at any point during this experience?

✴ Could you have spent more time in silence, darkness, and solitude?

✴ Where else could you go to eliminate distractions and spend time alone with God?

Closing: Repeat the adapted Prayer of Saint Patrick (see page 41) together.

9 In View of a Rainbow

"I have placed my bow in the clouds; it will be the symbol of the covenant between me and the earth" (Genesis 9:13).

Scripture: Genesis 9:12-15a

Theme: God Restores and Redeems

Supplies: You will need a supply of drawing paper and color pastels (or stock paper and crayons or markers).

Overview: God restores us during life's toughest moments. But we must pray for eyes to see the rainbow. This worship experience should take place outside shortly after it has stopped raining, while a rainbow is visible.

Opening Words: Say something like, *"A rainbow is one of God's fascinating creations that is utterly simple in design— light shining through water—but is awe-inspiring and imaginative to view. Rainbows fascinate children and adults alike. How many times have you said or heard, 'Oh look! There's a rainbow!'*

"We all know the story of Noah and the ark. As the turbulent days of the flood subsided, God used the rainbow as a symbol of God's covenant to restore the land and God's people and never again to destroy all life on earth with water. Being restored means being made new."

Invite the youth to reflect on these questions:

✳ What situations and relationships in your life have been trying and turbulent?

✳ How has God reached out to you and restored you during these troublesome times?

Sing Praise: (see note on page 6)

✳ "From the Rising of the Sun" (anonymous)
✳ "Lord I Lift Your Name on High" (Rick Founds)
✳ "Here Comes the Sun" (George Harrison)

Scripture Reading: Read aloud, or ask a youth to read aloud, **Genesis 9:12-15a.**

Activity: Look! There's a Rainbow!

Hand out the drawing paper and coloring supplies. Ask youth to use the whole page to draw the rainbow as they see it. When they have colored their rainbows, ask them to write on each color words that reflect some of the difficult and turbulent times in their lives—times when they needed to be restored by God. Under the rainbow, ask youth to write words that reflect a hope for restoration and new life.

Invite youth who wish to show and talk about their drawings. Then place all the drawings side by side on the ground, so that together they create a rainbow that reflects your group.

Closing: Ask youth to stand around your collection of rainbow pictures, leaving room for one person to also stand in the middle. Allow other youth to shout praises and thanksgivings for that person. Repeat, inviting each person in the group to stand in the middle. After God has been thanked and praised for each person in the group, ask for a volunteer to close in prayer.

10 Under a Starlit Sky

"'Look up at the sky and count the stars if you think you can count them.' He continued, 'This is how many children you will have'" (Genesis 15:5).

Scripture: Genesis 15:1-6

Theme: God's Dream for Us

Supplies: You will need a roll of wax paper or sheets of construction paper, pencils or a hole punch, and markers.

Overview: God's dream for our lives is far more grand than anything we wish for ourselves. As your youth gather under a starry nighttime sky, they will imagine God's dreams coming true in their lives.

Opening Words: Say something like, *"During the time of Abram (who later became Abraham), having a large family was very important. The family carried forward a father's name and legacy. It was a big deal to have children and an even bigger deal to have sons. Abram was getting older and so was his wife Sarai. Because of their age, Abram had already begun to think that he wouldn't have a child to carry on his name and estate. Because Sarai knew how important it was to Abram, and because she too had given up hope of bearing her own child, she encouraged Abram to have a child with her servant Hagar.*

"But God had different plans for Abram and Sarai. While gazing at the same stars as we are tonight, God spoke to Abram and said, 'Count the stars if you can.' And then God laid out a plan for Abram's life and legacy: He would live a much longer life than he imagined;

he would indeed have children born to his wife Sarai; and his descendants would be more numerous than the stars in the sky."

Sing Praise: (see note on page 6)

❋ "Deep Enough to Dream" (Chris Rice)
❋ "Come and Fill Our Hearts" (Taizé)
❋ "Surely God" (Andrew Dreitcer)

Scripture Reading: Read aloud **Genesis 9:12-15a.**

Activity: Reach for the Stars

Hand out the wax paper and markers. Ask the youth to look through the paper at the stars and to plot stars that are significant to them (perhaps the brightest ones). Don't limit the number of stars they can plot. After a few minutes, suggest youth spend some time in prayer, focusing on the dreams God has for them and their lives.

As your prayer time winds down, ask everyone to write one dream for each star plotted. Remind youth that in God's promise to Abram, each star represented a person in his family that God would use to bless him. In the same way, the stars your youth have plotted should represent their hopes for ways God might bless your group, community, or world. Give everyone plenty of time to dream and write. Then allow each person to share at least one of his or her dreams with the group.

Closing: Ask youth to spend a few minutes praying over their "stars" and dreams. Then ask them to combine their stars by taping them together in a quilt-like fashion. Find a place to hang the stars, then shine a light behind them to illuminate all of your group's dreams. Close by singing a favorite worship song.

11 In a Green Pasture

"He lets me rest in grassy meadows; he leads me to restful waters; he keeps me alive" (Psalm 23:2-3).

Scripture: Psalm 23

Theme: Rest and Peace

Supplies: You will need blankets, camp chairs, and baby oil.

Overview: Psalm 23 is often used at funerals because it assures us of God's presence and protection during life's darkest times. To gain a greater appreciation for this psalm, take your youth to a "green pasture" like the one mentioned in verse 2. Since most teens don't spend a lot of time in open pastures, heighten their senses by asking them to take a deep breath of fresh air, listen for the sounds of wind and water and birds, and observe any wildflowers growing in the field. You'll direct them in *lectio divina* using **Psalm 23** and then invite them to be anointed with oil on their heads.

Opening Words: Say something like, *"Psalm 23 is one of the most popular and familiar passages in the Bible. It is frequently read at funerals because it assures us that God walks beside us in dark times, comforting us and protecting us. The psalmist writes of God allowing him to lie down in 'green pastures.' Today we're going to claim this 'green pasture' as holy ground, rest in the peace of knowing that God is present with us, and feel the anointing oil on our heads."*

Sing Praise: (see note on page 6)

✳ "Surely God" (Andrew Dreitcer)
✳ "Come and Fill Our Hearts" (Taizé)
✳ "Open the Eyes of My Heart" (Paul Baloche)

Scripture Reading: Read aloud **Psalm 23**, or ask a youth to do so. There may even be youth in your group who can recite the Scripture from memory.

Activity: Rest in the Pastures

Spread out some blankets and/or set up camp chairs throughout the area. Ask the youth to find a space where they can be comfortable. If the weather is appropriate, suggest the youth take off their shoes and socks and feel the grass under their feet. Once everyone is settled, claim your space as holy by calling the youth to a time of prayer and meditation. Explain that you will lead a *lectio divina* (sacred reading) exercise by reading the psalm several times and singing some praise choruses in a chanting, repetitive style. Follow this format or any other that feels comfortable to you:

1. Read aloud or sing **Psalm 23**.
2. Be still for five minutes.
3. Read aloud or sing **Psalm 23**.
4. Be still for five minutes.
5. Read aloud **Psalm 23**.

Encourage the youth to lie in the field. Invite them to feel God's presence and to listen for God's still, small voice as it may whisper to them. During the stillness, ask the following questions to help youth focus their thoughts:

* How does it feel to lie in the field and be in God's presence?
* What does it mean for your cup to overflow?
* What does the feast that God has prepared for you look like?
* What does it feel like to dwell in the house of the Lord forever?

Closing: Say something like, *"Shepherds wiped oil on their sheep's heads to soothe and heal wounds; it was one way they cared for them. The psalmist writes that God anoints our heads with oil: God cares for us and soothes our wounds. As we close I'm going to wipe oil on your foreheads as a symbol of God's loving care."*

Move around the group and wipe a small amount of oil on each person's head. As you do, say a prayer of blessing, asking God to walk closely with him or her for all the days of his or her life.

12 At a Farm or Garden

"Remain in me, and I will remain in you" (John 15:4a).

Scripture: John 15:1-17

Theme: Being Part of the Kingdom

Supplies: Ask everyone to bring a camera, or create small groups in which at least one person has a camera. If possible, use actual cameras instead of cell phone cameras, since you may want to compile the photos in a youth group reflection book or a small art gallery. Also, if possible, bring along a laptop computer.

Overview: All of God's children are rooted in God's love and grace and can grow and bring life to others. You will use this time at a farm or garden to help youth observe the real-life connection between vine, branches, and fruit (see **John 15:5**).

Opening Words: Say something like, *"Life is cultivated here in this garden or on this farm; it does not just magically appear. All food has a 'grounding' in the roots of the plants it grows on and in the mineral-rich soil. During biblical times, everyone was intimately familiar with the practice of growing food for personal consumption or for the sale of goods and services. So when Christ taught using analogies associated with gardening and farming, his listeners could easily apply these parables to their lives.*

*"Christ teaches that we are rooted in him: He is the vine; we are the branches (see **John 15:5**). He urges us to remain connected to him to receive nourishment through the vine and to bear fruit. Without this nourishment we will wither and die.*

"The garden or farm is a place where we can observe this real-life connection between vine, branches, and fruit. Farmers and gardeners work hard to make sure that their crops have the nourishment and resources they need to bear fruit. As believers we also want to bear fruit and to live fruitful lives with and for God. So what is it that connects us to the 'vine'?"

Encourage responses and facilitate discussion about ways to stay connected to God.

Sing Praise: (see note on page 6)

✸ "I Am the Vine" (John Michael Talbot)

Scripture Reading: Read aloud **John 15:1-17.**

Activity: Camera Macro Project

Say something like: "We are going to do a prayer activity in which we observe and chronicle the intricate details of objects found around this garden or farm. The pictures we take with our cameras will illustrate our connection to God. I want everyone to wander around the garden or farm and take 'macro' photos that show how plants in this garden or farm grow, receive nourishment, and bear fruit. Macro photography is a form of photography in which you take close-up pictures to capture an object's detail and subtle beauty. To take good macro photos, you need to pay very close attention to the smallest parts of objects and the very tiniest details. Then use your camera's focus and zoom functions to take the best photos that you can. As you take your pictures, be in a spirit of prayer, remembering that Christ is the vine that nurtures us and enables us to bear fruit."

Note: Your youth most likely will not have ideal camera equipment for macro

photography. Don't worry too much about photo quality; instead encourage them to pay attention to detail and reflect on the Scripture.

After about an hour, call the group back together to discuss their reflections on the experience. If possible, plug the cameras, or their memory cards, into a laptop and look at each youth's pictures. Ask:

✳ What was your favorite image to capture on camera?
✳ What did you learn about God by taking a close look at the plants in this farm or garden?
✳ How has this experience helped you better understand the importance of staying connected to God?

In the coming days, use the participants' photos to create a computer slide show, a photobook for the youth room, or a gallery of prints. Also, save the photos for use during other worship times.

Closing: Lead youth in the following litany prayer.

LEADER: Lord Jesus Christ, Son of God, Vine of Life
ALL: Be the root of our life so that we will bear fruit.
LEADER: Lord Jesus Christ, Light of our world, cause us to grow in your light.
ALL: Be the root of our life so that we will bear fruit.
LEADER: Lord Jesus Christ, Bread of Life, nourish us as we grow.
ALL: Be the root of our life so that we will bear fruit.
LEADER: Lord Jesus Christ, Living Water, rain down on us so we can thrive.
ALL: Be the root of our life so that we will bear fruit.
LEADER: Lord Jesus Christ, You are the Vine and we are the branches.
ALL: Be the root of our life so that we will bear fruit.

Bonus: On a Trail

"On that same day, two disciples were traveling to a village called Emmaus, about seven miles from Jerusalem" (Luke 24:13).

Scripture: Luke 24:13-32

Theme: Pilgrimage With God

Supplies: Bring along a journal for each youth (this could be a notebook or several blank sheets of paper stapled together) and pens or pencils.

Overview: Our life with God is meant to be a pilgrimage. Sometimes, though, we act like tourists. Instead of walking with God all of the time, we stop in for a quick tour at our convenience. You will lead your youth on a "slow walk" to help them understand the importance of paying attention to what happens along their individual journeys of faith.

Opening Words: Say something like, *"In the movie* Cars, *there is a great scene where two of the cars are driving leisurely along a country road that passes through an old town. The road takes them through some amazing landscape as well as winding turns, which is fun for the cars. At one point the cars look over the top of a hill and see the interstate, packed with other cars speeding past without even noticing the magnificent countryside.*

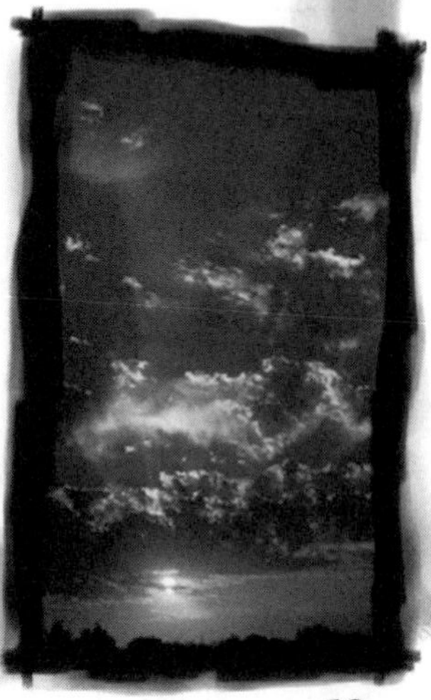

"Maybe you have a similar story. Maybe you've been on a family trip to a park or museum or historical site where most family members were tourists, but one person was making a pilgrimage. Let me explain: Tourists glance at exhibits and attractions; they take some pictures

and buy some souvenirs. Some tourists are along simply for the ride and become bored if they stay in one place too long. Pilgrims, on the other hand, relish every moment. They absorb every sight, sound, and smell; they read every historical placard; they speak with reverence about everything they see and experience; and they don't understand why others aren't as interested as they are.

"This difference between tourists and pilgrims is seen not only on family trips but also on our journeys with God. We can go along for the ride, reluctantly and passively, or we can cherish every step, sight, and experience along the way.

"Think about the places you go during a day. Think about where you travel on vacation. Think about the time you spend at school or work each day. How much of life passes you by? Who are the people that you pass by? What are the normal and unique places that you pass without truly seeing them.

"**Luke 24** tells about two disciples who set out on a seven-mile-long trail. They were so focused on their destination that they totally missed what was happening around them. They walked along that trail with Jesus, their Lord and teacher, yet didn't even notice who he was. They were like tourists zooming along an interstate. When Christ revealed himself to them, they realized what they had been missing all along the way."

Sing Praise: (see note on page 6)

* "Open the Eyes of My Heart" (Paul Baloche)
* "I Will Follow" (Chris Tomlin, Jason Ingram, Reuben Morgan)

Scripture Reading: Read aloud **Luke 24:13-32.** Emphasize that the disciples were walking and apparently not paying attention to anything, including Jesus' presence with them.

Activity: A Slow Walk

Before you set off to walk the trail, ask the group to write in their journals about the type of things they miss when they focus only on getting from one place to another and not on what happens along the way.

Give instructions for a "slow walk." The slow walk is meant to totally abandon the compulsion to finish first or rush to the end. The walk isn't about finishing; it is about the beauty, the revelation, the understanding, and the growth one encounters along the way. Encourage your youth to be deliberate in their slowness. Help them literally to stop and smell the roses.

As you walk together, lead your youth to take a certain number of steps forward and then a step back. For example, take twenty steps forward and then one step back. This helps to disrupt that finish-to-win-it approach. Don't worry about counting exact steps. Just walk a while and then step back a bit. Walk for ten minutes, then stop and talk for five minutes. Talk about something the youth passed while walking—leaves, bridges, creeks, animals, and so forth. Talk about the things that you don't usually notice, such as leaves and insects and rocks and flowers, then talk about the ways that God speaks to us when we slow down.

Closing: Psalms 120–134 are known as the Pilgrim Psalms. Read aloud **Psalm 121** as a closing prayer, and encourage the youth to study the Pilgrim Psalms for insight on living life as a pilgrimage with God instead of treating their faith as an occasional tourist destination.

✵ Bonus: In View of a Sunset

"Rejoice always. Pray continually. Give thanks in every situation because this is God's will for you in Christ Jesus" (1 Thessalonians 5:16–18).

Scripture: 1 Thessalonians 5:16-18

Theme: Life of Prayer

Supplies: None needed

Overview: Desert Father Abba Arsenius used the setting and rising of the sun as part of his daily prayer ritual. Each evening he turned toward the setting sun, raised his arms in prayer, and remained in prayer until the rising sun shone on his face the next morning. While youth probably shouldn't mimic Arsenius's all-night prayer habits, they should make prayer a way of life. You will gather your youth in time to conduct this worship experience during a sunset and introduce participants to prayer postures.

Opening Words: Say something like, *"Abba Arsenius, one of the Desert Fathers of our early church history (see 'In a Cave,' on page 39 for information about the Desert Fathers and Mothers), was so steeped in prayer that every evening he would turn his back towards the setting sun, raise his arms in prayer, and remain in that posture till the sun shown again on his face. He was also against sleeping. But that tradition died out (except at the occasional lock-in). So we're not going to stand here all night with our arms raised. But I do want you to imagine the sort of mental and physical dedication to prayer those actions would require.*

*"As Christians we are called to a life of prayer. **First Thessalonians** 5:17 tells us to pray continually, or without ceasing. Many times our prayers have a clear beginning and end; and in between we do all the talking. If you had a friendship in which you did all the talking, how great of a friendship would that be? Seriously, who is in a relationship where one person does all the communicating? No one. Our individual prayer life, which is our ongoing conversation with God, is part of a relationship. It isn't something we can do alone, or on our own terms.*

"Praying without ceasing isn't about starting and stopping a prayer over and over again; but it is about taking on an attitude that always reflects a relational conversation with God. We should always be looking towards God. We should always be listening to God. We should always be attuned to how God is working in the world. Abba Arsenius took the time from sunset to sunrise to attune himself to God's voice."

Sing Praise: (see note on page 6)

✳ "From the Rising of the Sun" (anonymous)

Scripture Reading: Read aloud 1 **Thessalonians** 5:16-18 or call on a youth to do so.

Activity: Practicing Prayer Postures

Say something like: *"We are not going to turn our backs to the sunset today, but in the example of Abba Arsenius, we are going to take on a prayer posture as the sun sets.*

"Prayer postures have been a part of our faith traditions since the beginning. A kneeling prayer position reflects the posture of Christ in the Garden of Gethsemane. Some church

fathers would lie prostrate (on their faces) or kneel as a posture of humility. And some Roman Catholic and Orthodox congregations worship using different postures throughout a service. We're going to adopt a posture during this sunset and praise the One who has created it."

Ask the group to spread out so that everyone has room to move, but not so far away that you cannot be heard. Instruct students to hold up their arms in a position of praise and prayer, for as long as they can. If their arms become tired, they may switch to kneeling or praying with open hands. Change the prayer posture as needed, but continue with prayer postures until the sun sets on the group.

When the sun has set, pause and allow youth a moment to reflect on the posturing experience. Then ask:

✳ How did this experience heighten your awareness of God's love and presence in new ways?

Closing: Read aloud **Psalm 134** as a closing prayer:

> All you who serve the LORD:
>   bless the LORD right now!
> All you who minister in the LORD's house at
>   night: bless God!
> Lift up your hands to the sanctuary and bless
>   the LORD!
> May the LORD,
>   the maker of heaven and earth,
>   bless you from Zion.
>   Amen.

Chapter 3
Worship
With Awareness

Sometimes the most meaningful worship moments come in the most unexpected places. This chapter is a collection of experiences to use during ordinary fellowship events such as camping trips, amusement parks, sports events, backyard parties, and so on. Use these worship experiences to help youth find God in the most unexpected and ordinary of places.

13 At a Rest Area

"Come to me, all you who are struggling hard and carrying heavy loads, and I will give you rest" (Matthew 11:28).

Scripture: Matthew 11:28-30

Theme: Resting in Jesus

Supplies: You'll need a few (three or four) empty backpacks.

Overview: If you're near a rest area, it's probably because you've been on a trip of some kind. Use this worship experience on your way home from a trip when your group is tired and can identify with what it feels like to be weary and burdened. You'll help the youth identify the burdens in their lives and symbolically toss them into a bag, then leave with Jesus and walk away free of those burdens.

Opening Words: Say something like, *"We have traveled many miles. We left behind the routine of our daily lives, but we carried with us the emotional burdens and stresses that never leave our minds. We have worked and played and lived in community; now we are returning home to school and work and family and church. We are tired and weary, but we are Jesus-followers and he promises to take our burdens upon him. He offers the rest for which our souls long. So we're going to pull over at this rest stop, give our burdens to Jesus, and leave for home with a lighter load."*

Scripture Reading: Read aloud **Matthew 11:28-30** or ask for a volunteer to do so.

Activity: Letting Go

Most rest areas have picnic tables, so gather your group around a picnic table and set out a few empty backpacks. Explain to the youth that they will trade in their burdens for Jesus' comfort and presence.

Now ask the youth to spend a minute thinking of the burdens they carry around every day. Then instruct them to look around the rest area for rocks, sticks, or other heavy objects that would represent those burdens and to fill the empty backpacks with their symbolic "burdens." When the backpacks are full, call the youth back and again gather around the table.

Say something like: *"These backpacks are now full of the burdens that we carry around every day: We worry about what's going on at home. We worry about what's going on at school. We worry about our grades. We worry about being popular. We worry about being successful. We worry about being loved. We worry about work. We worry about injustice and oppression. We worry about what we see or hear in the news. We carry a heavy load of burdens. But you know what? Jesus promises that following him means that we can be free from those burdens. When we seek Jesus for the rest and comfort and presence that we need, he frees us from the weight of our burdens and gives us the hope and joy and peace that allows us to live a life of faith and trust instead of worry and despair.*

"Now we're going to wear these backpacks that represent our burdens. And we're going to be reminded of Jesus' words as we remove the backpacks and feel the weight coming off. Then we're going to walk away from this place feeling free of our burdens and full of Christ's joy and peace."

Ask for a volunteer to wear all of the backpacks at the same time. As you read aloud **Matthew 11:28-30** again, instruct him or her to slowly remove each backpack. Repeat this activity, with each person who is able taking on the weight of the backpacks while you read aloud the Scripture. Or, you may want to call on students to read aloud the Scripture for one another. After each person has put on and taken off the backpacks, read aloud the Scripture passage one final time.

Sing Praise: Ask for suggestions of a favorite praise song to sing. Choose one that youth may continue to sing after they are back on the bus.

Closing: Stand at the door of the van or bus and say this blessing over the youth as they board: *"May your burdens melt away as you put your faith in Jesus. May you find him to be all that you need. May his burden be lighter than anything you've ever experienced. May you find rest for your weary soul. Amen."*

14 At a Campground

"Just like a deer that craves streams of water, so my whole being craves you, God" (Psalm 42:1).

Scripture: Psalm 42

Theme: Feeling Lost and Alone

Supplies: Ahead of time, print **Psalm 42** on the left-hand side of a sheet of paper, making a copy for each youth you expect. Take along these copies and pens or pencils.

Overview: We can feel lonely and melancholy whether we are alone in the wilderness or in the middle of a busy city. No matter how many people surround us, we can still feel like we're in the middle of a forest without a clue as to how to find our way out. It even can feel like everyone and everything is against us. As you spend time at a campground with your youth, you will take them to the middle of a wooded area and help them imagine what the writer of **Psalm 42** might have been feeling and thinking. Youth will rewrite the psalm and memorize the verses that speak loudest to them.

Opening Words: Say something like, *"Here we are—out in the middle of the woods. All we can hear is the wind in the trees and the animals rustling in the leaves. We are all alone. Sometimes loneliness feels like this, like being lost in the woods. Other times, even though we feel alone, we appear busy as bees, keeping up appearances to convince everyone that we're fine. But on the inside we feel disconnected from God and others. Today we're going to pray with the psalmist who*

wrote, 'Just like a deer that craves streams of water, so my whole being craves you, God.' We're going to sink into this psalm and learn what it means for us today."

Sing Praise: (see note on page 6)

☀ "As the Deer for Flowing Water Longs" (Stephen Iverson)

Scripture Reading: Read aloud **Psalm 42**. To experience the Scripture lesson, ask the youth to spread out and find a spot with some space to become comfortable. They should move apart, but stay within earshot of you. Explain that you will read the psalm three different times, using the practice of *lectio divina*. (You may have led *lectio divina* as a part of Experience 11, "In a Green Pasture" on page 47.) This experience of *lectio divina* differs from that one, though both are reflective meditations on Scripture.)

The first time you read the Scripture, youth should listen to the psalm just as it is, simply allowing the words to fall on their ears. The second time you read they should listen for words or phrases that jump out at them—those lines that make their heart leap or that ring true for them. The third time, they should listen for the verses that most clearly express any longing in their hearts—words that feel like prayers they might have written themselves. Allow a few minutes of silence between readings and remind students what to listen for before each reading.

After the final reading, pause for a few more moments of silence and then say something like: *"Just like the deer longs for water in these verses, our hearts long to be filled with the presence of God. Often we are consumed by the activity of our daily lives—school, work, sports, music, family stuff, friends,* and on and on it goes. In the middle of all the chaos, we can become lost in ourselves. We can forget that God promises to be with us, to fill us with the Holy Spirit, and to satisfy our longings. We can all relate to this psalmist's cry. He is lonely. He feels beaten up. He feels lost. But he resolves to trust in God. He even gives himself a pep talk: 'Hope in God! Because I will again give him thanks, my saving presence and my God' (verse 5). Sometimes we need to remind ourselves to place our hope in God. One way we can do that is to memorize Scripture. When we are confused about who or whose we are, when we feel lost in the world, when we feel like everyone is out to get us, we can call to mind the words of the psalms and receive encouragement and assurance of God's presence."

Activity: Psalm 42 Redux

Hand out the pens and printouts of **Psalm 42**. Explain that youth should rewrite the psalm using their own words. Once they have paraphrased the psalm, they should read and think about each line and consider the verses that resonate most with them. Encourage youth to memorize those verses by writing them on the back of the page and repeating them silently. (They should write the biblical version of these verses rather than their paraphrase, though it wouldn't hurt to memorize the paraphrase also.) After about thirty minutes of reflection and memorization time, reassemble as a group.

Closing: Ask youth to form a circle, then move around the circle and allow youth to recite the verse(s) they chose to memorize. Say a closing prayer asking God to fill the youth with hope and a constant awareness of God's presence. Also pray that when youth are lonely or feel depressed, they will look to God for comfort and healing.

15 At a Park

"Every good gift, every perfect gift, comes from above" *(James 1:17).*

Scripture: James 1:17

Theme: Play

Supplies: Bible

Overview: Sometimes we need to take time out to remember our childhood—the freedom we once felt to run and play and be ourselves. As children most of us were more open to joy and lived with wide-eyed wonder at the love and beauty of God, though we wouldn't have described it like that at the time. Most days, and in most situations, youth are expected to act like short grownups. With this worship experience, give them the gift of a few hours to act like children and enjoy friendship, fellowship, and the warm sunshine as wonderful gifts from God.

Opening Words: Say something like, *"Here we are at a park in our city. When was the last time you guys went to a park? Do you remember how much you loved to play at the park when you were kids? I bet your parents took you to the park on Saturday mornings or arranged playdates with your friends during the week. But as you grew older, it wasn't cool anymore to want to swing or slide.*

"Now you drive by the park on your way to and from other places. Most days you have to use your 'inside' voices and act properly all day—but today, in the park, you can let loose! Let's play like children and experience the joy we knew so freely when we were younger."

Sing Praise: Sing some old-school children's worship tunes, such as the following (see note on page 6):

* ✳ "I've Got the Joy, Joy, Joy Down in My Heart"
* ✳ "I've Got Peace Like a River"
* ✳ "Al-la-la-la-la-la-le-lu-ia"
* ✳ "Deep and Wide"

Scripture Reading: Read aloud **James 1:17**. Ask the youth to shout out good things in their lives (*family, friends, french fries*, and so on.) Talk about the truth that all good things are gifts from God—good things like joy, sunshine, exercise, friendship, and even play.

Activity: Playtime

Explain that, as an act of worshiping God, youth will spend time playing. Say something like: "*In the same way that singing, praying, and Scripture reading can be acts of worship, so can enjoying the beauty of a day and the good friends that God has given you. In an act of praise and thankfulness to God for friendship and beautiful days, we're going to play in the park.*"

Begin by leading youth to play some organized games like hide-and-seek and freeze tag. Then, without any structured activities, allow the group some time to swing, slide, climb, and simply enjoy the day with friends. After an hour or so, call the youth back together for a closing song and prayer.

Closing: Sing together "Jesus Loves Me." Then hold hands and thank God for the gift of play and friendship. Ask God to help youth remember to live each day with joy.

16 At a Bonfire

"Because of Christ, we give off a sweet scent rising to God, which is recognized by those on the way of salvation—an aroma redolent with life" (2 Corinthians 2:14, THE MESSAGE).

Scripture: 2 Corinthians 2:12-17

Theme: Being the Fragrance of Christ in the World

Supplies: Gather all the supplies needed to start a bonfire (such as firewood, kindling, and matches), along with a stick of incense for each person.

Overview: This experience will demonstrate to youth what it means to be the fragrance of Christ in the world. The smell of fire is strong and causes those near it to smell of smoke, since the smoke sinks into fabrics. During this experience (at a campground or other facility where you can safely and legally build a bonfire), you'll use incense to create a waft of sweet-smelling smoke that will help youth imagine themselves being a fragrance that fills the air everywhere they go.

Opening Words: Say something like, *"Tonight we gather around this bonfire in community and to reflect on our faithfulness to Christ. Have you ever noticed how long you smell like smoke after standing around a bonfire? Your clothes usually need a few washings to get the smell out, right? I want you to think about something Paul said in 2 Corinthians— that our lives can be like the fragrance of Christ that we leave in the air everywhere we go."*

Sing Praise: The atmosphere lends itself to singing, so sing these and other favorite songs as long as time and interest allows (see note on page 6).

✳ "Light the Fire" (Bill Maxwell)
✳ "From the Rising of the Sun" (anonymous)

Scripture Reading: Read aloud 2 **Corinthians** 2:12-17.

Activity: Spreading the Aroma

Hand out a stick of incense to each person. Say something like: *"In our Scripture passage, Paul talks to us about the great task of living for Jesus and pointing others to him. He described his work as spreading the aroma of Christ everywhere he went. His kindness, clarity about his life's mission, hope in Jesus Christ, and joy in the work was infectious. People wanted to know this Jesus who had changed Paul's life.*

"Is that what your life is like? Do you leave a scent of love and joy and hope wherever you go? Do you love to talk about what Jesus is doing in your life? Do you point others to Christ with your words and your actions?

"Stick the end of an incense stick into the fire. Let it catch fire, then quickly blow it out so that it smokes. As we pray together I want you to imagine that this fragrance and smoke represent your passion for sharing Jesus with everyone you meet. People should know that you follow Jesus because you leave an aroma of love and joy and peace wherever you go."

Lead the responsive prayer on the following page as the youth hold their incense sticks.

LEADER: Jesus, your love makes our lives worth living.

YOUTH: Fill us with your sweet-smelling fragrance that leads others to you.

LEADER: We want everyone to know, everywhere we go, that your love is better than life.

YOUTH: Fill us with your sweet-smelling fragrance that leads others to you.

LEADER: Let our lives, our words, and our actions tell the story of all you've done.

YOUTH: Fill us with your sweet-smelling fragrance that leads others to you.

LEADER: Be pleased as the fragrance of our love for you rises to heaven.

YOUTH: Fill us with your sweet-smelling fragrance that leads others to you.

Closing: Invite the youth to toss their incense sticks into the fire as an act of declaration and commitment that they will leave the sweet fragrance of Christ's love everywhere they go.

17 At An Amusement Park

"Then Jesus went to work on his disciples. 'Anyone who intends to come with me has to let me lead. You are not in the driver's seat; I am. Don't run from suffering; embrace it. Follow me and I'll show you how. Self-help is no help at all. Self-sacrifice is the way, my way, to finding yourself, your true self. What kind of deal is it to get everything you want but lose yourself? What could you ever trade your soul for?'" (Matthew 16:24-26, THE MESSAGE).

Scripture: Matthew 16:24-26

Theme: The Great Adventure

Supplies: Provide a mini spiral notebook and small pencil for each person. Make sure the notebooks are pocket-sized so that youth can keep them handy during the day.

Overview: What better place to talk about the great adventure of following Jesus than at an amusement park. Sometimes life can feel like a roller coaster with all its ups and downs. We may also feel like we're in the log jam and either stuck or about to take a plunge. Other times we can feel like we're experiencing a free fall—straight down with no bottom in sight. The tilt-a-whirl reminds us that time just keeps spinning and spinning; we can either enjoy the ride or focus on the twirling and be miserable. At an amusement park we choose our ride! We sign up for the excitement. We know it's mostly safe—yet gives the illusion of risk—and it is so worth it!

As you spend the day in the park, you'll help your youth make connections to their faith lives. You'll have a time of prayer before everyone disperses to enjoy the day's activities. Then, you'll gather again at the end of the day to praise God for fun, for the invitation to the journey, and for the friends with whom you share this adventure-filled life.

Opening Words: Say something like, "*When Jesus calls us to follow him, he invites us on the ultimate adventure. We go along for the ride, allowing him to sit in the driver's seat, and he leads us to some amazing places. As you look around this park, you'll see rides that remind us of the great adventure of our life in Christ. There are ups and downs and spins and turns. Sometimes we are scared, but still we don't want to get off the ride. Other times we run for the 'chicken' exit because we lack the trust in Jesus that is required.*

"*Following Jesus won't cost you the price of any tickets or season passes, but it will cost you some trust, some faith, some courage, and ultimately your need to be in control.*"

Scripture Reading: Read aloud **Matthew 16:24-26**, preferably from *THE MESSAGE*.

Activity: Practicing Prayer

Hand out mini spiral notebooks and small pencils. Allow youth to gather in small groups naturally, but make sure that no one is left out. Explain that they should practice prayer as they stand in line, ride the rides, and eat the unique park food. Throughout the day they also should look for ways that every ride or activity can relate to their lives with God. At every attraction they choose, youth should take a minute to assess the ride (its twists and turns and element of thrill) and compare it to following Jesus. Then they should write in their notebooks a one- or two-sentence prayer that reflects this comparison. For example, they might write: "Lord, life with you can be like riding this roller coaster. Sometimes I feel like it's taking forever to move forward. Sometimes I feel like I'm holding on for dear life. Help me hold on to you when life is upside-down and crazy." Explain that, at the end of the day, youth will read their prayers together. Say a prayer of protection over youth before they head out into the park. Be sure to tell them where and when to meet in the afternoon.

At the end of the day, when your group has reassembled, invite youth to talk about their favorite parts of the day. Encourage them to tell stories about their feelings of thrill, fear, and fun. Then talk about their experience of praying throughout the day. As they talk, draw comparisons between the rides and their relationship with God.

Closing: Ask each person to read aloud at least one of his or her prayers. Then read aloud the Scripture passage again. Invite your youth to either commit or recommit themselves to a life of great adventure with Jesus. Pray this prayer of blessing or one of your own: *"Dear Father, Watch over these young people who seek to follow you. Help them to live their lives with joy— even through the ups and downs and spins—and to say 'yes' to Jesus when he calls them to take risks. Amen."*

18 In a Backyard

"But the legal expert wanted to prove that he was right, so he said to Jesus, 'And who is my neighbor?'" (Luke 10:29).

Scripture: Luke 10:25-37 (parable of the good Samaritan)

Theme: Who Is My Neighbor?

Supplies: You will need at least three tables (depending on your group size). Also provide a small bell and the supplies needed for each prayer station (see page 75).

Overview: At your next backyard barbeque or swim party, youth will think about their neighbors and the needs that might be in their own backyard, literally. They will reflect on the parable of the good Samaritan and pray for eyes to view everyone they meet as neighbors. You will set up prayer stations around the yard and give youth opportunities to meditate on loving God and loving others.

Opening Words: Say something like, *"Sometimes we are so caught up in our personal lives that we don't even notice the needs of people around us. Today we're going to talk about having eyes to see the world as Jesus does—eyes that see those in need of care or help that we can offer."*

Sing Praise: (see note on page 6)

* "Ubi Caritas (Live in Charity)" (anonymous, traditional)
* "Everywhere I Go, I See You" (Rich Mullins)
* "Mighty to Save" (Hillsong)

Scripture Reading: Slowly and deliberately read aloud **Luke 10:25-37**, making sure youth understand Jesus' words.

Activity: Eyes to See

Ahead of time set up prayer stations around the yard using the instructions below. Depending on your group size, you may want to set up multiple tables for each prayer station so that no one has to wait. Copy the instructions for youth (see page 76) on one or more pieces of paper, or duplicate the instructions and post the appropriate instructions at each table.

Table 1 Preparation: Cover the table with a world map. Set out several Bibles and thinline markers in a variety of colors. Youth will write prayers on the map. Post instructions (see page 76).

Table 2 Preparation: Provide Bibles, phone books, and highlighters. Youth will find as many hospitals, jails, homeless missions, food pantries, and poverty ministries as possible in the phone books, then highlight the listings and pray for the workers in the facility and for the persons served by the facility. Post instructions (see page 76).

Table 3 Preparation: Set out drawing paper and markers. Youth will draw a picture or map of their individual streets and all the homes around them, then pray for each of these families and for God to show them (the youth) how to be good neighbors. Post instructions (see page 76).

Closing: After the youth have rotated through the prayer stations, ring the bell to reassemble, then sing another worship song. Pray, asking God to give your youth courage to stop and help when they see someone in need.

TABLE 1 YOUTH INSTRUCTIONS: PRAY FOR THE WORLD

1. Read the parable of the good Samaritan: Luke 10:25-37.

2. As you look at the world map, reflect on the idea that a neighbor can live both next door and around the world. If a country or region jumps out at you, write at that location on the map a prayer for the people who live there. Pray for God to show you how to be a neighbor to people everywhere.

TABLE 2 YOUTH INSTRUCTIONS: PRAY FOR YOUR COMMUNITY

1. Read the parable of the good Samaritan: Luke 10:25-37.

2. Flip through the phone book and find listings for hospitals, prisons, homeless shelters, food pantries, poverty ministries, and other help organizations. Mark these listings with a highlighter and pray for the people who work at the facilities as well as the people who receive their services. Ask God to show you how to be a neighbor in your community.

TABLE 3 YOUTH INSTRUCTIONS: PRAY FOR YOUR NEIGHBORHOOD

1. Read the parable of the good Samaritan: Luke 10:25-37.

2. Draw a picture or map featuring your house and the surrounding homes on your street. Evaluate your strengths and weaknesses as a neighbor. Do you show care, love, and hospitality to those who live near you? Pray for each family on your street or block and pray for God to show you how to be a good neighbor.

Worship Feast: 25 Experiences of God's Great Earth

⊗ Bonus: At a Sports Event

"The goal I pursue is the prize of God's upward call in Christ Jesus" (Philippians 3:14).

Scripture: Philippians 3:12-14

Theme: Trying Versus Training

Supplies: Duplicate copies of the blank award certificate on page 80, one for each youth expected. (Or, you can print your own certificates from the Internet. There are several sites that offer free templates.)

Overview: The apostle Paul was probably an athletic guy. He likened his spiritual growth to running a race for a prize (and once compared it to boxing, see **1 Corinthians 9:26**). Of course the prize he was seeking was Christlikeness—not a cash prize or a gold medal. As you meet to watch a sports event, help your youth imagine training for a life with Christ in the same way that athletes practice and train for their sports. What do you think would happen if a group of guys who loved football but had no real training or conditioning went up against an NFL team? They wouldn't stand a chance. In the same way we must train for discipleship. We don't just "try" to follow Jesus; we are instructed to train our minds and hearts.

Opening Words: Say something like, *"Before we go into the stadium, I want us to think about all of the training that goes into an event like this. For years these players have worked and sacrificed and pushed themselves, sometimes beyond what they believed they could do. They have done anything necessary*

to reach their goal—whether that goal involves beating a rival team, winning a championship, or just getting on the scoreboard. Regardless of their goals or of how much they love the game, they can't expect positive results without training.

"In the same way, we can't just 'try' to follow Jesus. We must train for discipleship through disciplines such as prayer, worship, Bible study, and small-group accountability. We have to practice our faith to become more and more like Jesus."

Scripture Reading: Read aloud **Philippians 3:12-14**, or ask a youth to do so.

Activity: Pressing On

Ask the youth to think about what they believe Paul meant by "the prize." Ask:

* What does Paul mean when he says he hasn't reached the prize yet?
* How does he press on toward his goal?
* What is his goal?
* How is his determination similar to that of an athlete?
* What do Paul's words in this Scripture say about our commitment to a life with Christ?

Say something like: "*Think about the training regimens of the athletes you're about to watch. How does their training compare to your training as a follower of Christ? Are you committed to a life of prayer and Bible study? of growing in your relationship with Christ? Salvation is a gift to you from God, and there's nothing we can do to earn it. But we can work to become more and more like Jesus.*

*"Think about it in this way: When you are struggling with a particular sinful temptation, you probably try really hard not to give in. The only part of you involved with the trying is your will. You will yourself not to commit that sin. But our will isn't always strong enough to stand up to temptation, so we continue in the struggle. That's why Paul also told us to be 'transformed by the renewing of [our] minds' (**Romans 12:2**). It takes some effort to renew our minds. We press on toward our goal by training—doing the work that will make our hearts and minds more sensitive to the movement of God until we become like Christ, until we are transformed."*

Hand out the blank award certificates and explain that you will collect these in a minute before youth go into the stadium. Say something like: *"I want each of you to take home a blank certificate and place it where you'll see it periodically. The certificate will serve as a reminder that you have a goal, or prize, in your Christian life—to be more and more like Jesus. Take a minute now to write on the back of the certificate a personal training plan for the coming week. Maybe you'll commit to five minutes of prayer each day. Maybe you'll memorize a psalm. Set a few goals that will be acts of pursuing 'the prize' of becoming more like Christ."*

Closing: After a few minutes, collect the certificates. Before you head in, pray for the safety of the players on the teams who are playing today. Pray that God would give your youth dedication to the life of discipleship like that of an athlete to his or her sport. (Remember to give youth their certificates before they leave for home.)

certificate of Award

Presented to:

_____

for

_____

_____

"Don't be conformed to the patterns of this world, but be transformed by the renewing of your minds." —Romans 12:2

✸ Bonus: At a Mall

"But the fruit of the Spirit is love, joy, peace, patience, kindness, goodness, faithfulness, gentleness, and self-control. There is no law against things like this" (Galatians 5:22-23).

Scripture: Galatians 5:22-23

Theme: Hurrying

Supplies: None needed

Overview: If you go to a mall and watch the people in the cars in the parking lot and those going in and out of stores, you'll notice that most of them look like they are hurrying. Many of us know the feeling of rushing here and there, afraid that the world will end if we don't make it to the store for that "one more thing." We are angry when someone cuts us off at the intersection or steals "our" parking spot. We push our way through to the fastest-moving line at checkout. We call ahead to pick up supper so we don't have to wait. Somehow our lives take on a rhythm of "hurry here, hurry there" instead of a schedule marked with peace and joy-filled moments. To hurry is often a choice we make; to *not* hurry is also a choice we can make.

You can help your youth to think critically about hurrying through their teen years and their already full schedules. But after high school they'll decide for themselves how to survive the hustle and bustle of a busy life. Will they see each moment as a step in their daily walk with God, or will they be consumed and overwhelmed by activity, straying from the path of faith?

In this worship experience youth will walk in pairs or small groups around the outside of the mall, praying silent prayers for people who look overworked, hurried, angry, or otherwise in need of prayer. Assign an adult volunteer to each group. The youth should not make a spectacle of themselves and should be as discreet as possible, walking slowly and looking for ways to show kindness to others as an act of protest to hurrying through life.

Opening Words: Say something like, *"In our culture we value productivity. The busier we appear, the more we've got going on; the more we look stressed and overworked—the better. If we take our time and eliminate unnecessary stress—if we do only what we can comfortably do—then we appear lazy or unambitious. But why do we do that to ourselves? For approval? From whom?*

"How many of us have yelled at someone who cut us off at an intersection? How many of us have had terrible thoughts about someone who took 'our' parking spot? How many of us swoop into that open checkout line when the attendant calls out, 'I can help someone at register 4.'? How many of us race to the mall determined to get a bargain before anyone else? And how many of us act like we're the most important people to ever park or walk through the doors?

"Today we're going to slow down. We're going to pray that God would convict us of our self-absorption and arrogance as we pray for the busy people here at this mall."

Scripture Reading: Before you give instructions and send out the youth, read aloud **Galatians 5:22-23.** Explain that when we live our lives in the Spirit, as Paul teaches, we set aside our greed and pride and selfishness and demonstrate the spiritual fruits that have grown in us:

love, joy, peace, patience, kindness, goodness, faithfulness, gentleness, and self-control. These qualities should define our lives as followers of Jesus Christ—not fighting for parking spaces and rushing through our days without noticing anyone or anything that can't help get us where we're going or what we need.

Activity: Undercover Kindness

Divide the youth into pairs or small groups. Explain that youth should seek out ways to demonstrate the fruit of the Spirit to people around the mall. They should consider their actions to be humble protests of a culture of hurry and worry. They should go out of their way to show kindness, gentleness, and love. Instruct them to pray as a group for people who seem hurried, rushed, or overwhelmed. Set a one-hour time limit for their kindness spree, and designate a time and place to regroup.

When all the groups or pairs have returned, debrief the experience using questions such as:

* What was your overall impression of this experience?
* How hurried did people appear to be?
* Did you see anything funny or out of the ordinary?
* How did it feel to go out of your way to show kindness?
* How did people receive your kind acts?
* What prayers did you say?
* How does this experience make you think about your personal life? Are you too hurried? How can you slow down?

Say something like: *"When we follow Jesus, the Holy Spirit continually transforms us so that we become more and more like Christ. We know that the Spirit is working in us*

when we bear the Spirit's fruit. Our challenge is to get out of the way and allow the Spirit to lead us in a life of kindness, gentleness, self-control, love, and joy."

Closing: Ask the youth to stand in a circle and hold hands. Invite volunteers to pray individual, single-sentence prayers, perhaps for someone they observed on their prayer walk. Then close by praying for the group: "God, thank you for this time to pray for others. Help us to slow down and to eliminate unnecessary hurry and worry in our lives. Free us for joyful obedience in our daily faith walk. Amen."

Note: If you have time and the budget, spend some unhurried fellowship time together and see a movie while at the mall.

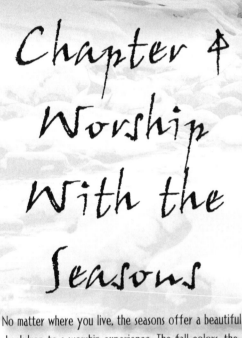

Chapter 4
Worship
With the
Seasons

No matter where you live, the seasons offer a beautiful backdrop to a worship experience. The fall colors, the winter snows, and the budding flowers in spring are all symbols of the creativity, attention to detail, and beauty of our Maker. They also point to hope—that the sun will come up again, that the seasons will change, that the promise of spring follows the darkness of winter. Use the beauty of the seasons to help your youth worship the beautiful God who made them.

19 In a Snow Fall

"The angel said, 'Don't be afraid! Look! I bring good news to you—wonderful, joyous news for all people. Your savior is born today in David's city. He is Christ the Lord. This is a sign for you: you will find a newborn baby wrapped snugly and lying in a manger'" (Luke 2:10-12).

Scripture: Luke 1–2

Theme: Christmas

Supplies: You will need a Bible and an MP3 or CD player, if possible.

Overview: Contemporary Christian artist Audrey Assad has written a Christmas song titled "Winter Snow" that is sure to become a favorite. She writes about the way Jesus came into our world, reminding us that he could have arrived with fanfare and hubbub, but that was not what God had in mind. She describes Jesus' arrival like a winter snow—soft, quiet, and slow. There were no trumpet blasts or national celebrations. And there was no immediate rise to power. After growing in Mary's womb for nine quiet months, he was born in an ordinary barn. And he grew up like other children—until it was time for him to usher in his kingdom. Sometime during this winter season, worship with your group as the snow falls and ponder the truth that God's ways are often not what we expect.

Ask one of your student musicians to learn the song and sing it for the group. Or purchase a copy of the song and be prepared to play it during your worship time. (You can find "Winter Snow," performed by Audrey Assad and Chris Tomlin, on Tomlin's *Glory in the Highest: Christmas Songs of Worship* album.)

Opening Words: Say something like, *"Most of us know the story of Jesus' birth. From an early age we learned the story through Bible storybooks, Christmas pageants, and Advent calendars. We know that angels spoke to shepherds, that Jesus was born in a manger, and that wise men traveled to bring him gifts. Today we're going to ponder the way that Jesus—the Prince of Peace—came into the world.*

"Typically, if a king were coming, people would prepare. There would be fanfare and ceremony and pomp and circumstance. People would leave work early or stop whatever they were doing and go to see the king. The people of Jesus' day were awaiting the coming of the Messiah, and they expected him to arrive like any other king.

"But that's not God's style. God chose an ordinary girl to carry the King in her belly for nine months. God chose for Jesus to arrive quietly. And, in the beginning, God chose to tell only a few groups of people. God chose for Jesus to make his appearance much like a winter snow."

Sing Praise: (see note on page 6)

✳ "In the Bleak Midwinter" (Christina Rossetti)

Ahead of time enlist a student musician to sing or teach the group the words and melody to Audrey Assad's "Winter Snow," or play it on an MP3 or CD player.

Scripture Reading: Read aloud **Luke 1:26—2:20** and repeat **Luke 2:10-12** at the end. Emphasize the significance of God coming to earth as a baby.

Activity: Winter Snow

Designate three station areas for meditation. You don't need tables, but you will need to provide instructions at each of the areas.

Station 1: Snow Angels

Students will meditate on the angels bringing the news of Jesus' birth to the shepherds. Instead of couriers and telegrams and government decrees, this king was announced to ordinary (and probably smelly) shepherds in the middle of a field. Ask the youth to meditate on this part of the story as they make snow angels.

Station 2: Catching Snow Flakes

Students will meditate on the quiet, slow way that snowflakes fall from the sky. Youth should catch snowflakes on their hands or their tongues. Invite them to look on their sleeves and examine the intricacy of fresh snowflakes and be amazed at the wonder of God.

Station 3: Writing in the Snow

Students should meditate on the fact that Jesus came to earth as a baby. Remind them that he knows every experience we have in life. Jesus is "God with us." As they ponder the baby king, ask the youth to write the words "for unto us a child is born" in the snow.

Closing: Close your worship experience by singing or listening once more to the song "Winter Snow." Then, pray this prayer or one of your own: *"Emmanuel, God with us, we are in awe of the way you work through the unexpected. You gained our attention by sneaking into this world through a humble girl. We worship you this Christmas and praise you for coming to know us, to save us, and to love us. Amen."*

20 Among Budding Trees and Flowers

"As for what was planted on good soil, this refers to those who hear and understand, and bear fruit and produce—in one case a yield of hundred to one, in another case a yield of sixty to one, and in another case a yield of thirty to one" (Matthew 13:23).

Scripture: Matthew 13:1-23

Theme: Good Soil

Supplies: You will need a a small clay pot for each student, bags of potting soil, packets of seeds (choose plants that grow easily and are easy to maintain so that youth will see success), colored thinline permanent markers, a filled watering can or jar, and Bibles.

Overview: After a long, dark winter our bodies and spirits ache for signs of spring. Those rare warm days remind us that the earth is about to wake up and come alive. Flowers and leaves are on their way. Daylight lasts longer, giving buds more time to soak up the sunlight. Take your students outside where there are obvious signs of spring, such as a garden or a park. Students will plant seeds in a pot while you lead them to pray that God would bring about new life in them as they grow like the spring flowers.

Opening Words: Say something like, *"Aren't you tired of bundling up and layering and shoveling and scraping? I long to feel the warm sun and linger in its light, don't you? In the same way these buds around us are sitting*

up a little higher, reaching toward the sun to get that extra hint of sunlight. Very soon these buds will burst open, and the earth will wake up with color and light. Right now we are waiting—in the hoping season.

"Today we're going to plant seeds that we'll care for and nurture until they become beautiful flowers. As we do that, we'll think about the soil of our lives. Are we soft, rich, and ready for seeds of hope, peace, and love to grow in us? Or, are we hard and dry and unable to nurture growth?"

Sing Praise: (see note on page 6)

✳ "Hymn of Promise" (Natalie Sleeth)
✳ "Above All" (Michael W. Smith)
✳ "Everything Glorious" (David Crowder)

Scripture Reading: Read aloud **Matthew 13:1-23**, or ask several volunteers to read a few verses at a time.

Activity: Planting Seeds of Hope

Give everyone a pot, some dirt, some seeds, and at least one colored thinline marker. Also point out the watering can. Explain that you will read some instructions and lead youth in each step of planting the seeds (see below), then pause while students reflect and pray and work with the dirt and plants.

LEADER INSTRUCTIONS

Read aloud each of the following steps, then pause for a few moments while your youth complete the instructions. (Pause for as long as your scheduled time allows.)

✳ Think about your favorite Bible verses. What is one verse that gives you hope or helps you feel connected to God? Write the verse on the outside of your pot to remind you of your growth in Christ as your seeds sprout and grow.

✳ Now pour some dirt into the pot. Create a hole in the center for the seeds and save some dirt to cover them. Think about the nature of the dirt—it's smell, it's earthiness—typically something you'd want to avoid, right? But when you're planting, you need the minerals in the soil. Think about your heart as soil for God's truth and will in your life. Is your soil (heart) hard and impenetrable? Or, is your soil (heart) soft and nourishing like your potting soil, ready for seeds to be sown? As you work with the dirt, pray that God would make your heart soft for God to bring about fruit in your life.

✳ Place your seeds in the center of the dirt. Consider that the seeds represent hope, faith, peace, righteousness, gratitude, and love. These seeds will grow into beautiful flowers and bless those around them with beauty. How will your life in Christ become a blessing to those around you? How might hope, faith, righteousness, peace, gratitude, and love become like flowers growing from your heart?

✳ Cover the seeds with dirt and lightly water them. Take a minute to pray that God would grow in you, that even now you would bear seeds of hope and love that will bloom as you water them with prayer, Bible study, time with God, and time in fellowship. Pray that God would water your seeds with the Holy Spirit and protect them from harsh elements. Place this flower pot in the light of a window and let it remind you to pray as you watch it grow.

Closing: When everyone is finished planting and praying, ask each person to talk about the verse that he or she wrote on the pot. Talk about what it means to bear fruit. Ask the youth in what areas of faith they would like to grow and bear more fruit.

Now ask everyone to set their planters in the middle of the table and then gather around them in a circle. Pray this prayer or one of your own: *"Lord, the time has come again for flowers and leaves to spring forth. We have been in hibernation, but here comes the sun! We thank you for the way you hide your Word in our hearts and show us more and more of yourself as we seek you. Lord, we pray that our faith would grow like the seeds in these planters. Come and water us with the Holy Spirit so that the fruits of a life with you would grow and bless those around us. Make us good soil that you can use for good works. Amen."*

21 In the Fullness of Spring

"But the angel said to the women, 'Don't be afraid. I know that you are looking for Jesus who was crucified. He isn't here, because he's been raised from the dead, just as he said. Come, see the place where they laid him'" (Matthew 28:5-6).

Scripture: Matthew 28

Theme: Easter

Supplies: Ahead of time ask each youth to bring a sleeping bag or picnic blanket, a journal (notebook), and a Bible. Be sure to take along some extras of everything, as well as pens for everyone.

Overview: Every year as Easter approaches, we anticipate hope breaking forth from the empty tomb. Those three days before the Resurrection were like a long, dark winter; but hope and joy burst open on that first Easter morning. Like the field of flowers and blooming trees that you'll gather in or nearby, hope came crashing into our world: There would be no more death for those who follow Jesus. The risen Lord is alive and with us forever. Help your youth visualize hope as they gaze at the beauty of flowers blooming around them.

If possible, meet in the garden of someone who will allow the youth to cut some blooms to take home (perhaps a church member). If you meet in a public place, check with park management, explain your need, and ask if there is an area where your youth might be able to pick at least one bloom each. However, you will be able to

lead this worship experience even if your setting doesn't allow you to cut fresh flowers.

Opening Words: Say something like, *"The week leading up to the Crucifixion was an emotional roller coaster for Jesus and his disciples. The Crucifixion itself probably seemed like it would last forever; but surely those moments and days of sadness that followed also seemed neverending to the disciples. But God would not allow their sadness and gloom to last for long. Hope was coming! On that third day, the women visited the tomb and found it empty. Maybe the garden was blooming as bright as this field. Maybe it was like that scene in the* Wizard of Oz *when everything changes from black and white to full color. Maybe hope came alive for the women and for the disciples as they discovered that Jesus had risen, that the sadness was over, and that joy had arrived.*

"Today we're going to gaze on this field of springtime beauty and pray that God would burst into our lives with hope and that Easter wouldn't be just a story we hear once a year, but the very story we tell with our lives."

Sing Praise: (see note on page 6)

☀ "In Christ Alone" (Stuart Townend)
☀ "Christ the Lord Is Risen Today" (Charles Wesley)

Scripture Reading: Hand out Bibles and ask the youth to help you read aloud **Matthew 28**, each person reading one verse at a time. Talk about what the women must have thought when they arrived at the tomb: What were their emotions? What might they have said to one another?

Now ask youth to think about what those first disciples might have thought upon hearing that Jesus was not in the tomb: Would they have assumed that God was doing a new thing? Would they have continued to despair? Did they immediately want to go and look for Jesus?

Activity: He Is Alive!

Ask the youth to move apart and find a place among the flowers where they can reflect in silence and solitude. Remind them to take their picnic blankets and notebooks, pens, and Bibles.

First, suggest the youth spend a few quiet moments just enjoying God's beautiful spring creations: the flowers, the soft breeze, the smell of grass, the birds chirping. Next ask them to read **Matthew 28** a few times, imagining themselves in the story. After reading and imagining themselves arriving at the empty tomb, youth should record their thoughts and reactions in their journal. Ask them to think about how they feel on the way to the tomb, what they see around them in the garden, what they do when they notice that the tomb is empty. Finally, the youth should write about what the empty tomb means for their lives today.

After thirty minutes, reassemble as a group to talk about the experience. Ask for volunteers to talk about and read aloud some of their thoughts, prayers, and writings. What surprised them about the story? What do they believe the empty tomb means for their lives today?

Closing: Sing again "Christ the Lord Is Risen Today," or another favorite praise chorus, and close in prayer. If allowed, tell each person to pick a flower as a reminder of this experience.

22 In the Heat of a Summer Day

*"He shouted, 'Father Abraham, have mercy on me.
Send Lazarus to dip the tip of his finger in water and
cool my tongue because I'm suffering in this flame'"*
(Luke 16:24).

Scripture: Luke 16:19-31

Theme: Judgment

Supplies: Bibles

Overview: The story of Lazarus and the rich man is a
difficult story to hear. On the one hand, the rich man gets
what's coming to him and Lazarus is rewarded—just the
kind of justice we like—the kind where the underdog wins
in the end. But, it's hard to hear the rich man crying out to
be saved from the fire of hell. Father Abraham basically
says, "Too bad, so sad, rich man!" We're so accustomed to
talking about God's love and mercy that it's painful to
hear stories about judgment. But it does remind us that
God is serious about showing love and mercy. We cannot
love God and withhold love from others or be stingy or
selfish or care only about what will benefit us in the end.
God demands generosity and that we care for and minister
to the poor around us.

Help your youth feel the heat and consider the seriousness
of failing to care for the Lazarus's in our lives. Provide an
opportunity for them to think about their level of
generosity. Are they free with their time, their care, their
love, and their possessions—or are they stingy and selfish
at times?

Opening Words: Say something like, *"Today we're going to learn how serious God is about being generous, merciful, and compassionate. Sometimes we focus so much on God's mercy and love that we fail to appreciate the seriousness of God's judgment. Our story is about a rich man who was stingy, selfish, proud, haughty, and thought only of himself. A poor man named Lazarus longed to eat the scraps from the rich man's table. The parable paints a picture of the rich man yelling up from the fire of hell to Abraham and Lazarus. He begged Lazarus to dip down with some water to cool his tongue. He begged Lazarus to go and warn his living family about the fires that awaited them. But Abraham, from heaven, basically says to the rich man, 'Too bad, so sad, rich man. You had a great life and kept it all to yourself. Lazarus had a miserable life and is being rewarded now. If your family wanted to believe they would have by now.'*

"It's painful to imagine this story happening because the rich man is literally being sent to hell with no mercy. The fire of hell is so tormenting that he wishes he could warn his family. Today we're going to wrestle with God's judgment and imagine being on either side of this story.

"It's hot outside today. Imagine how hot we are now compared to the fiery heat the rich man felt. He was desperate for a drop of water to cool his mouth. He was parched—to say the very least. We're going to put ourselves in this story and see what truths it holds for us."

Sing Praise: (see note on page 6)

* "Wonderful, Merciful, Savior" (Dawn Rodgers, Eric Wyse)
* "Beautiful One" (Tim Hughes)
* "Days of Elijah" (Robin Mark)

Scripture Reading: Allow the youth to take turns reading aloud **Luke:16:19-31**. When they're finished, ask the following questions:

✳ Where is the sin in this story? mercy? judgment?
✳ Do you think the rich man was punished too harshly? Why or why not?
✳ Why, do you think, did the rich man not receive mercy?
✳ What do you think this parable has to say to us today?

Activity: Too Bad, So Sad

Obviously you won't want to stay out in the heat of the day for very long, but ask the youth to imagine themselves in this story by creating a skit that conveys its meaning. They may want to retell the story as it is in the Scripture, or they may want to retell it in their own words and present it as a roleplay. Encourage them to be creative and to think about what they believe God wants to communicate to us through this parable.

Divide the youth into small groups of three (so that there are people to play the roles of the rich man, Lazarus, and Abraham). If your numbers require you to create some groups of four, the fourth person in those groups could act as a narrator. Give the students about thirty minutes to create their dramas. Then allow each group to perform its skit for the others. Talk about whether each group emphasizes a different truth from the story, or if they are similar. Encourage applause.

Closing: Affirm each group's creativity, then pray for God to give your youth generous hearts and eyes to see the world as Christ sees it.

23 A Late Summer Night

"Taste and see how good the LORD is!" (Psalm 34:8).

Scripture: Psalm 34:7-9

Theme: Resting and Enjoying God's Good Things

Supplies: You'll need vanilla ice cream, root beer, mugs, spoons, and straws. Also provide some camp chairs and picnic blankets. If possible, light a campfire.

Overview: Summer nights are great, aren't they? The heat fades along with the sun. The moon reflects a beautiful glow while casting shadows. And the stars come out to twinkle hello. Encourage your youth to drink up the lazy summer days like refreshment from God. These long days can be like a sabbatical for youth—time to check out for a while—to sleep in, to relax, to unwind, to grow into the next season of their lives. Take this opportunity to relax with your youth on a summer night. Sit outside and soak up those extra minutes of God's nighttime creation.

Opening Words: Say something like, *"During the school year we are bound to our daily routine. We are up with the alarm clock and then to bed at a reasonable hour. We have only so much time to spend with our friends because of school assignments, sports, work, and other obligations. We stress over grades and school drama. And while we're grateful for the opportunity to learn and grow, we are tired of doing the same things day after day and week after week.*

"Summertime is a sabbatical, a time when we can take a break from the heavy-duty stuff and relax in the warm sunshine, then stay up late on long, summer nights. Today we are going to celebrate the God who created day and night, summer and winter, sun and moon. We are going to stay up late, sit outside, and enjoy time with one another as an act of worship to the God who created us for community."

Sing Praise: (see note on page 6)

* "From the Rising of the Sun" (anonymous)
* "Great Is Thy Faithfulness" (Thomas Chisolm, William Runyan)
* "Everything Glorious" (David Crowder)
* "O Praise Him (All This for a King)" (David Crowder)

Scripture Reading: Read aloud **Psalm 34:7-9** a few times. Talk about what it means to "taste and see" that God is good. What are some ways your group can experience God's goodness?

Activity: Sharing Community

Say something like: *"Have you ever considered that just being together like this, loving one another, living in community, is an act of worship? Did you know that God loves it when we enjoy God's wonderful creations—like long, summer nights? God loves it when we take time to celebrate the good things in our lives, to recognize a season of resting and refueling, and to soak in the loveliness of God's creation. That's what we're going to do tonight. We are going to worship God by hanging out, relaxing, and soaking in some of God's good gifts."*

Prepare a table with the ice cream, root beer, mugs, spoons, and straws. Invite the youth to make root beer floats. Spread out some blankets and camp chairs. If possible, light a campfire. Consider this an act of caring for your students—make them comfortable and encourage them to relax.

Once everyone is settled with their floats and comfortable in their spots, ask the following questions to facilitate conversation:

* What is your favorite thing about summer?
* What are some of your crazy summer vacation stories?
* What do you miss about school during the summer?
* How can spending nights like this, enjoying our time with Christian friends, be a form of worship?

Closing: Close your evening by singing "From the Rising of the Sun" a few times. Then lead this prayer or one of your own: *"Lord, you are so good. We have tasted and seen your goodness tonight. Thank you for long, summer nights that give us time to relax, to enjoy fellowship with Christian friends, and to unwind from a busy school year. Thank you for knowing what we need and providing so perfectly for us. Help us remember to pay attention to your goodness throughout the year. Remind us to worship you by the very way we live our lives—in community, in celebration, in work, and in rest. Let us sleep in peace this night. Amen."*

24 When Autumn Leaves Are Falling

"About that time . . . a complaint arose. Greek-speaking disciples accused the Aramaic-speaking disciples because their widows were being overlooked in the daily food service. The Twelve called a meeting of all the disciples and said, . . . 'Brothers and sisters, carefully choose seven well-respected men from among you. They must be well-respected and endowed by the Spirit with exceptional wisdom. We will put them in charge of this concern'" (Acts 6:1-3).

Scripture: Acts 6:1-7

Theme: Acts of Love and Service

Supplies: You'll need garden gloves, lawn-size garbage bags, and simple refreshments.

Overview: Plan to gather on a fall Saturday after most of the autumn leaves have fallen. Prior to your meeting, think about some of the elderly people in your church who might need help raking the leaves in their yards. Drive around and scout out the homes of some church members who could use a random act of love and help with their raking.

First, gather in the morning to thank God for the changing of the seasons and the season of harvest. Then visit several houses, helping to rake and bag fallen leaves and sweep sidewalks. At the end of the day, meet back at the church, your house, or another volunteer's house who has a yard with a lot of leaves. End the day in a playful way with youth enjoying time together by jumping and playing in the piles of leaves.

Opening Words: Say something like, *"When the leaves fall from the trees during autumn, it's a sign that the earth is making its move toward winter. But before the cold weather arrives, we can celebrate the harvest and all the bounty that God's good earth provides. Part of the beauty of the season is the changing color of the leaves and watching them drift from the trees to the ground. But, if you help with the leaf-raking at your house, you know that there is a lot of work involved in the cleanup. So today we're going to spend time outside enjoying the beauty of a fall day while visiting some elderly friends and raking their leaves and sweeping their sidewalks. As we work with our hands to help others in service, let's be in an attitude of prayer for the persons and families we are serving."*

Sing Praise: Sing praise songs familiar to your group that emphasize reaching out to others in a spirit of love or that praise God for the beauty of creation. (Continue to sing later as you work together.)

Scripture Reading: Ask a volunteer to read aloud **Acts 6:1-7**, then say something like: *"The apostles were so wrapped up in preaching about Christ that they weren't meeting the day-to-day needs of the people in the church, particularly the widows. Knowing that they couldn't overlook these needs, they appointed seven people to be in charge of service. This tradition of service is still an important part of the church's work. Today we're going to serve members of our congregation who have needs that aren't being met."*

Activity: Autumn Leaves Are Falling

Before you begin, gather in a circle and pray that you would sense God's presence among you and your youth and the families you help as you do your work throughout the day.

Closing: After your last act of raking, head to the church yard or someone's yard who has lots of leaves and enjoy some fellowship time. Encourage the group to rake the leaves, then jump and play in them. Also serve some simple refreshments (maybe hot chocolate and cookies) and celebrate a day of good work.

When your time together begins to wind down, gather for a closing prayer and thank God for the beauty of the fall day, the strength to do good work, and God's presence with you always.

25 On a Windy Day

"Suddenly a sound from heaven like the howling of a fierce wind filled the entire house where they were sitting" (Acts 2:2).

Scripture: Acts 2:1-13

Theme: Pentecost

Supplies: You'll need a plain kite for each person and some thinline permanent markers.

Overview: The story of the first Christian Pentecost (see Acts 2:1-41) tells of how the Holy Spirit came down "like the howling of a fierce wind" and filled the apostles. The Greek word that is translated "Holy Spirit," *pneuma* (NOO-muh), also means "wind" or "breath." Help your youth experience the Pentecost story by gathering to tell it outside on a very windy day. Provide kites, on which youth will write individual prayers, and then watch their prayers soar in the wind.

Opening Words: Say something like, *"We're going to take advantage of this windy day as an opportunity to reflect on and experience the story of Pentecost. The Bible says that, on Pentecost, the Holy Spirit came down with 'a sound from heaven like the howling of a fierce wind.' We often associate the Holy Spirit with wind. In fact, the Greek word that is translated 'Holy Spirit,' pneuma (NOO-muh), also means 'wind' or 'breath.' As we feel the wind on our faces today, let's pray to be filled with the Holy Spirit to do God's work in the world."*

Sing Praise: (see note on page 6)

☀ "Holy Spirit, Rain Down" (Russell Fragar)
☀ "Come, Holy Spirit" (Mark Foreman)

Scripture Reading: Ask for some volunteers to take turns reading aloud the Pentecost story from **Acts 2:1-13.**

Activity: Go Fly a Kite

Talk with youth about the first Pentecost. Help them imagine the Holy Spirit coming down in such a tangible and incredible way. Ask them to imagine the feeling of being filled with the Holy Spirit in that setting and the excitement of a Christian movement being born. Ask the youth, "What would it be like if we were so filled with the Holy Spirit that thousands of people around us came to believe in Jesus?"

Now ask the youth to reflect on these questions and thoughts as they write the Scripture verse **Acts 2:2** on their individual kites, along with a brief prayer for them to be Jesus to people they meet. Before flying the kites, allow any youth who wish to read aloud their prayers.

After youth have read aloud prayers, help students get their kites in the air (if they need help). Once everyone has their kite up and flying, read aloud **Acts 2:1-13** again as their prayers reach upward. Then allow youth to have some fun simply running around and flying their kites.

Closing: As you prepare to leave, gather together and pray, asking God to fill your group with the Holy Spirit and to give all of you the strength, the courage, and the faith to tell the world about God's love and salvation in Jesus Christ.

❄ Bonus: On a Freezing Cold Day

"God issues his command to the earth—
   God's word speeds off fast!
God spreads snow like it was wool;
   God scatters frost like it was ashes;
God throws his hail down like crumbs—
   who can endure God's freezing cold?
Then God issues his word
   and melts it all away!
   God makes his winds blow;
   the water flows again" (Psalm 147:15-18).

Scripture: Psalm 147

Theme: God's Power

Supplies: You'll need hot chocolate and mugs or cups.

Overview: Cold days with no snow to look at or play in can seem pointless, can't they? But the cold weather can speak to the greatness of God. **Psalm 147** reminds us that God covers the sky with clouds and sends the rain to the earth. The psalmist celebrates that God is powerful and mighty and the Master of all seasons. Remind your youth of God's power on a cold day.

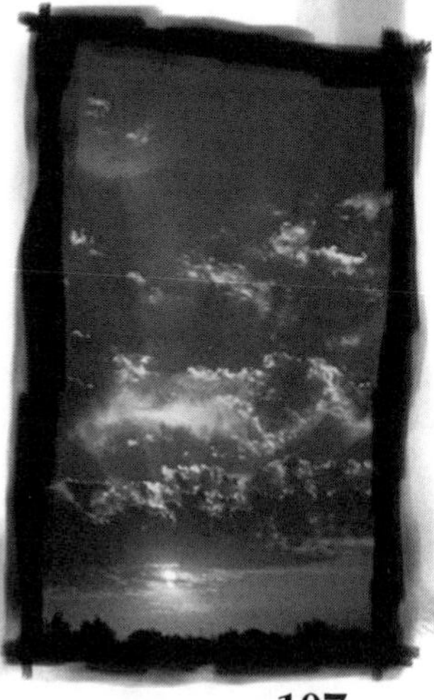

Opening Words: Say something like, "*In The Lion, the Witch, and the Wardrobe, the first installment of* The Chronicles of Narnia, *Lucy finds the kingdom of Narnia under the reign of the White Witch. The*

witch has decreed that it will always be winter—but never Christmas. The sky in Narnia under the White Witch was always gray, and the cold was nearly unbearable.

"Days like today can feel a bit like frozen Narnia. But if we look to the psalms, we'll discover that God is the God not only of warm, sunny days but also of the dark, frozen days—days like today. A life with God carries with it the promise of hope. A life with God looks to God as the Maker and Giver and Lover of all good things. So this cold day is an opportunity to be amazed at the power of God, the Creator of our unique world. We're going to stay outside for only a few minutes, but while we're out there, I want us to truly listen to the words of the psalm and feel it like the chill on our cheeks."

Sing Praise: To warm up, sing lively songs of praise that mention sunshine and warmth. (If the weather outside is especially bitter, you might add some fun hand motions to get the blood flowing or skip directly to the Scripture reading.)

Scripture Reading: Read aloud **Psalm 147** a few times— slowly and deliberately.

Activity: Prayer Circle

Lead a domino-style prayer in which one person begins by saying one line of prayer and it continues around the circle, each person adding a line. Begin with the opening statements below and encourage youth to add one thought at a time.

Pray: "God, you are so great. We thank you for . . ." (*the first youth then takes over the prayer, naming one thing he or she is thankful for, then passes the prayer to the next person*).

When the prayer circle returns to you, pray: "God, you are strong and mighty. On cold days like these we remember . . ." (*the prayer moves around the circle again with each person naming one good and hopeful thing to remember on cold, dark days*).

Finally, pray: "Lord, this icy blast can cause us to lose hope that spring will ever come. Remind us that . . ." (*the prayer moves around one last time with each person naming one truth about God and life that makes them hopeful*). Then close the prayer with your personal words of assurance.

Closing: Read **Psalm 147** again, allowing God's Word to linger as you move inside. Serve some hot chocolate to help warm up youth.

Worship Feast
Resources

The WORSHIP FEAST series offers practical ways to meet the worship needs of postmodern youth and young adults and to help them experience God in a new way.

✳ *Worship Feast Lent and Easter*
Offers youth leaders an exciting alternative to other Lent and Easter worship fare.
Includes seven original Lent-themed worship songs on an audio CD along with printed lyrics and chords.
ISBN: 9780687643998 (Abingdon Press)

✳ *Worship Feast Advent and Christmas*
Offers youth leaders an exciting alternative to other Advent and Christmas worship fare.
Includes seven original Advent Christmas-themed worship songs on an audio CD along with printed lyrics and chords. ISBN: 9780687465422 (Abingdon Press)

✳ *Worship Feast Liturgical Dance—8 Easy-to-Learn Dances for Worship* (DVD)
Features step-by-step instructional choreography for liturgical dance for any skill level.
ISBN: 9780687643776 (Abingdon Press)

✳ *Worship Feast Readings—50 Readings, Rituals, Prayers, and Guided Meditations*
A collection of readings to use in creating meaningful worship, devotion, and prayer times for youth.
ISBN: 9780687741816 (Abingdon Press)

* *Worship Feast Services—50 Complete Multi-Sensory Services for Youth*
  Includes services for the various seasons, prayer and healing, discovering your spiritual type, graduates, and many more. ISBN: 9780687063673 (Abingdon Press)

* *Worship Feast Ideas—100 Awesome Ideas for Postmodern Youth*
  Ideas for creating your own services or incorporating multisensory worship elements into your existing services, including incense, silence, secular music, and more. ISBN: 9780687063574 (Abingdon Press)

* *Worship Feast Dramas—15 Sketches for Youth Groups, Worship, and More*
  Includes a variety of long and short skits field-tested with youth in real-life situations.
  ISBN: 9780687044597 (Abingdon Press)

* *Worship Feast Taizé—20 Complete Services in the Spirit of Taizé*
  Services offer meditations, song suggestions, prayers, and use of silence. Includes a split-track, instrumental music CD. ISBN: 9780687741915 (Abingdon Press)

* *Worship Feast Taizé Songbook*
  Includes 15 popular and easy-to-sing Taizé songs, featuring simple melody lines, guitar chords, and the text in English and other languages.
  ISBN: 9780687739325 (Abingdon Press).